DOGS WITH THE RIGHT STUFF

AUTHOR

PERRY CHARLES DODGE

To Amy with
fond respect.

Perry C Dodge

July 9th, 2003

This book is a work of fiction. Places, events, and situations in this story are purely fictional. Any resemblance to actual persons, living or dead, is coincidental.

ISBN: 1-4107-1101-3 (e-book)
ISBN: 1-4107-1102-1 (Paperback)

This book is printed on acid free paper.

1stBooks – rev. 01/16/03

CONTENTS

INTRODUCTION

"**Dogs' Con School**," answers: What is a Con Dog? Who teaches the class? Why? How can it benefit dogs or people?

"**Three Legged Ginger**," tells her amazing story before, during and after she suffered the loss of her back leg.

"**Flash the Fire Dog**," is an imaginative look at dogs teaching other dogs about life saving.

"**Creampuff the Cougar Dog**," tells about hunting a vicious, cunning and powerful creature with an exceptional dog.

"**The Gold Mine Dogs**," is a humorous and enlightening tale about two family dogs in a gold mine. The older dog teaches his playmate, (and the reader), about gold mining in the early twentieth century.

"**Buster the Proud Pomeranian**," whose story of loyalty and devotion is told in his view.

"**A Dog Named Zy**," is a heartwarming tale about a family dog who guards his peoples' things and braves year-around outdoor life in southeast Alaska.

"**Diamond Eyed Spot**," is an intriguing and humorous mystery about a family ranch dog that gets kidnaped for ransom.

"**Meet Woofer**," is packed full of gripping suspense and the numerous adventures of a dog that helps others and sometimes needs help.

<u>ACKNOWLEDGMENTS</u>

The author is grateful to the following persons for their ever-present efforts and encouragement:

GARY HUSTOFT, Oregon City, Oregon. He helped me keep my computer working and kept me from "killing" it.

DON CROCKETT, Roseburg, Oregon, the author of the mystery novel, "Buried in Stone." He kept me motivated and on-track.

MY WIFE, M. ANN DODGE, Roseburg, Oregon. I especially appreciate her insight, perspectives, editing expertise, and encouragement. Her unfaltering support has added immeasurably to this book.

"THANX" again to one and all, Perry.

I

DOG'S CON SCHOOL

Introduction

Learning should be fun and it is hoped that such will be the case with this writing. In an effort to inform the readers to the desired level without losing their interest, the writer uses humor in many of the examples in the text. To express what the animal thinks or would like to say, the thought is written like we would speak or write the same message. Or stated another way, we put words in the dog's mouth.

The Reader Needs to Know:

What is a Con Dog? The shortened term, "CON," means to CONvince or to gain CONfidence.

Who Teaches the Course? Older, fully trained and more experienced **SMART DOGS** teach younger dogs the fine art of *inspiring* humans to do the dog's bidding, while thinking it is the person's idea.

What do we mean by smart dogs? By now the reader surely knows that dogs need abilities far beyond our wildest imagination in order to even consider the tasks outlined above. It is already widely known that dogs have feelings and moods much like people. They have senses and knowledge that are foreign to us. For example, if a human dies in a remote place, they let other persons know with a mournful howl unlike any other. How can they possibly know what has happened? We don't know how, but they absolutely do.

For another example, any dog can be taught to count. Sometimes sheep herders teach their dogs to bring in a spoken or signaled number of sheep. The dog will deliver the specified number, and any remaining sheep will not join the movement. To be a smart dog, it must be able to do more than put one foot in front of the other. The extra smart ones can drive people crazy by playing tricks on them, such as hiding a prized possession, like a man's pipe or a lady's slipper. In the next story, *Ginger* was a great one to pull such stunts on her people, especially the children. If the person gets suspicious, most dogs can present a picture of total innocence, like a bratty kid. It seems logical that extra smart **student** dogs will try to con their instructors, but that may be easier said than done. When the SMART DOGS were learning to teach, that problem was probably dealt with.

What can the Student Dogs be expected to learn? They will learn *obedience* and *psychology*, and how to apply them to gain compliance with their suggestive thoughts. When the person refuses or ignores the suggestion, the lives of people or dogs may depend upon that person becoming **delighted** to comply.

Class Organization by Smart Dogs

First they must select the most promising dogs as students:
a. Pick the best temperament and disposition
b. Avoid aggressive or sourpuss attitudes
Next they must outline a training plan tailored to the introduction stated above, with emphasis on the italicized keywords *inspiring, obedience* and *psychology.*

Learning What Makes Them Tick

How can we tell their emotions? We can tell by their facial expressions and actions when they are sad, glad, mad or in just about any frame of mind experienced by humans. They communicate their feelings and thoughts among themselves in many ways that we don't understand. It may be less obvious but dogs and other animals feel the same things that we do. *Love* is plainly shown by a mother dog caring for her puppies. *Hate* and *anger* are obvious when the dog curls its lips, snarls or growls. They show hate by showing anger toward any creature that acts mean or hateful toward the dog, its human family or animal family, then you must keep your distance. *Fear* is usually shown by shaking, cowering and lowering the head and tail, also by mournful howling and begging attention. *Happiness* is readily recognized when a dog is riding in the family vehicle with its head out of the window on a hot summer day. If it could speak it might say, "Boy! This has to be the greatest feeling in the world!" That dog is in Heaven.

Instinct

Instinct is an automatic impulse in humans and animals, to satisfy basic biological needs, leading to a behavior that is purposeful and constructive. Perhaps a simpler definition of instinct is an inborn tendency to behave in a way characteristic of a species. When a mother dog gives birth to a litter of pups, she <u>instinctively</u> knows what must be done to care for their health and welfare. The newborn pups know where to nurse. Astonishingly, each pup knows where the correct nipple is and how to use it. They don't go to school for that. There is no credible evidence of any training being given by other dogs in this instance, despite the fact that the mother starts the teaching process soon after the birth of her litter.

Obedience and Psychology Training

Obedience and Psychology Training is initially part of the mother's teaching soon after her pups are born. The classes taught by the smart dogs probably start with an introduction to these subjects. In order to organize the class, teaching must begin with <u>obedience</u>. For them to teach their student dogs to con people, the use of psychology is required. Isn't this how teaching starts with humans?

Learning the use of psychology to con people is a lifelong project and it would take several books to cover the subject. One commonly used con stunt is to act so cute that the person can't resist accommodating the dog's wishes. In, *"Three Legged Ginger,"* which is the next chapter, she would roll over, sit up and beg, or lay her head on your knee and give you her extremely doleful look, which no human could resist. In, *"Flash the Fire Dog,"* he learns much more about **inspiring, obedience** and

5

psychology during his emergency rescue training. There are occasional references to these topics throughout this book.

The Teaching and Learning Process

The process probably starts and continues in much the same manner with dogs as with humans. At birth they seem to already know who their mother is and how to feed on her milk. Newborn dogs know when their mother calls and they soon learn to understand some of the things she wants them to do. When she goes away from the den they know whether to stay until she returns or to go with her when she leaves. The mother soon begins teaching them about the good things in the world and about things to avoid. She teaches them to play, to enjoy life and to develop the physical strength to defend themselves. She also starts training them about dangers, but this is continued throughout their life and is taught by many trainers.

In the story, *"Flash the Fire Dog,"* while teaching Emergency Search and Rescue, **The Boss** said, "I can't overstress the importance of getting people to see and understand your thoughts about what must be done, while thinking it is **their idea**." He also said, "In emergencies we must insure to convey the **correct** idea to people. We are blessed with the ability to share our thoughts and feelings with people without using speech like they do. As they would say, we **con** them. This is the key to inspiring the proper action. When it comes to our own actions, obedience is vitally important. We don't have the privilege to choose right or wrong in an emergency. We have enough smarts to know the right action and we must see that it happens that way. With that said, there is a fly in the ointment. Sometimes people fail to see the point of our messages. Then we must be prepared to justify what we did, or explain why we failed to deliver the message and **convince** those who needed to act. The stakes are high, inaction or wrong action often costs lives, maybe people's lives or dogs' lives." As we said earlier, "We must make them **delighted** to comply."

An example of dogs' intellect or power to reason and think is illustrated by this event. Some of the local farmers loved to take their dogs pheasant hunting in the fall. This time one of the kids rode in the back of the family pickup before and after the hunt. That day they hunted until after dark before they had their limit of game, by then the people and dogs were bone-tired. On the way home the dogs were laying in a circle in the pickup bed and were sound asleep. One of the dogs stirred, stretched and yawned, then moved, stepping on another dog's privates, and laid back down. The victim raised up and looked all around, but had no idea who was the culprit. He bristled his hair, growled, and bit every dog! Then he calmly laid back down.

The real world

Soon after the pups start learning to play one of the teacher-dogs will take them hunting in the wilds so they can learn about things like the smell of skunks and the feel of porcupine quills. If a pup is about as smart as the average sagebrush, he will avoid the next skunk or porcupine. Also, he will probably be leery of other creatures. If your family dog comes home with quills in his nose, someone needs to remove the quills without hurting the dog. That experience can be terribly painful and should be handled by a veterinarian if possible. Otherwise it should be done by an adult to minimize injury to the dog and lessen the chance of someone being bitten by the dog. The dog may wish he could say, "Hey buddy, you even touch my quills and I'll tie you in a bow knot!" The quills are like sharp needles and are hollow, with air pressure inside that pushes the barbs out from the sides. The barbs tend to catch on the flesh when you try to pull the quills out. The quills can be depressurized by cutting them in two, which eases the force pushing the barbs into the flesh. They should be cut far enough back to leave a place to grip them to pull them out. We repeat, take your dog to the vet if possible.

When the pups are being taught to hunt by the smart-dogs they learn to locate and overcome whatever game is available. Dogs are often involved in hunting the badger, bear, beaver, cougar, deer, duck, pheasant, rabbit, raccoon or any of a myriad of other species. The teachers must use the equivalent of a dialog to convey the ideas of how to hunt. For example they might say, "We suggest that you learn the different animals in your area, then don't take on the biggest and meanest one at first. Also stay away from some that are not very big, like badgers and beavers. Your area may have some rabbits that would be good to start with. Give some thought to your own size and how tough you really are. If you are a Toy Terrier, you'd better leave the heavy work to a better equipped dog. If you are a Dachshund, you are pretty darn tough. Nature made them low slung and strong as a bull so that they can challenge badgers and beavers which burrow under the ground. One last suggestion, before you start combat with any animal, **be sure you are ready!** It will be fighting for its life!"

Dogs don't enjoy it when they disturb a skunk. If your dog has been sprayed by a skunk you will know exactly what the smell is. The only known cure is to wait until January 49th for the smell to go away. You can figure that under arm deodorant won't be of much help. It might not be a good idea to let the dog in the house, especially if you still wish to live there. By the way, unlike with porcupine quills, your vet might not be too happy if you took your mutt to his clinic with a skunk's spray job. Your poor animal might laugh himself sick if you were that dumb. I suppose you should suit yourself.

Wild Dogs

Sometimes dogs organize a group of their kind and train them to hunt and attack other creatures in warlike ways. Little is known about the training process in this case except that they are often seen following practices similar to wolf packs. Both dogs and wolves are famous for preying on livestock and other animals. The important thing is to avoid letting our children interfere with the exploits of such packs of potential killers. If you are a child, don't bother them. They might have you over for supper. If people or property are at risk, do not try to stop the animals. Notify law enforcement or animal control personnel. They are trained and equipped to deal with such problems.

Parting Thoughts

Dogs with The Right Stuff is fiction and many of the ideas cannot be proven, but the author often writes what he thinks the dog thought, or would have said. The reader can learn from and enjoy the stories by deliberating or weighing what the dog may have thought or said. The following eight chapters tell the stories of nine dogs, five of which were real and the others imaginary. Can you tell which are which?

The various warnings in this story are intended to encourage the reader to use judgment and consideration during the care of your animal, or other animals. The hope is to keep you aware that there are always safety concerns for both the person and the animal. Being **alert** and **aware** are the first line of defense. These thoughts do not mean to avoid pets, and the pleasures they can add to your life, not to mention how human companionship can do the same for the animal. Do yourself a favor, get a pet and do all you can to make its life, and your life, wonderful!

II

THREE LEGGED GINGER

This is the laughable, heartwarming and yet sometimes heart breaking story of an affectionate, caring, life-loving, and cute Cocker Spaniel dog named Ginger. Her love for and devotion to her human family sets the standard for all family dogs. Ginger's feelings and the things she might wish she could say are expressed in writing below.

The story begins by telling how she became a three-legged dog, followed by her story before and after the dramatic event that would have challenged any other man or beast.

The Accident

Ginger had a long history of being an accomplished escapee. Sometimes when she was supposed to be somewhere, such as in the house, it might not have been her idea. She took great joy in both the escape and the freedom afterwards. On this occasion she was in the living room taking a nap on her doggy basket. The family mother was there at the time waiting for the kids to come in from school. At the sound of the school bus the mother started outdoors to meet it and when the door began to open Ginger was outside quicker than lightning. She ran out from behind a parked car, into the path of the bus. The driver stopped just as the back wheel was on her hind leg. The mother got the driver to move backward, off of the dog's leg and quickly went to her aid. Ginger didn't seem to be badly hurt but they took her to the veterinarian, just in case.

The vet examined her and said he thought she was OK, but he wanted to take some X-rays to be sure. When he came back out, he said, "Well young lady, it seems your dog is going to be fine. There are no fractures but I'd still like to keep her overnight. You can check with me in the morning and I'll let you know for sure." The next morning the mother was at the vet's as soon as they opened. When she saw the vet, he had a solemn look on his face that gave her a terrible dread of what was coming. He said, "I'm awfully sorry Mam, but Ginger has some very serious nerve damage and we are going to have to amputate her leg. With your permission we are ready to do the procedure." She asked, "What other choices are available?" He said, "If we don't remove the leg, she will suffer ever increasing agony until she dies." The shock of the vet's words were nearly more than the mother could bear and Ginger licked her hand to relieve her grief. When they were taking her to the operating room Ginger was wagging her tail. Later when they brought her back out she seemed real woozy but she didn't show any sign of being in pain. One of the technicians who assisted said, "I've never seen anything like Ginger, that little darling never whimpered. She is such a pleasure to work with."

That evening the mother took the family to see their pet and find out what was next. The vet said, "I'm totally amazed at Ginger's spunk and the way she is handling the change in her life. She is already getting around and managing to do the things she seems to wish to do. When you visit, please avoid touching her surgery area. Now I think you and your family can use some good news. Ginger will be ready and able to go home in the morning." When they entered the room, Ginger jumped up and licked the face of each visitor. She even played with them for a few moments. She got around by hopping with her back foot and she seemed to sense how to go about each task. Ginger thought, "Gosh it's sad that the family doesn't know how well I can manage to deal with this. At least I know they will be proud to see the results."

The next morning the mother picked her up from the vet's office and took her home. She was astonished beyond words at Ginger's playful and loving attitude, plus her high degree of intelligence in finding ways to do as she wished. Ginger and her family were really in heaven on earth. Ginger thought, "I sure hope I get to play outside today, it's so beautiful." The mother let Ginger out into the back yard where they could play and they both had a wonderful morning. Ginger went after her favorite toy which she had played with every since she had joined the family. Ginger thought, "Life can't get any better than this!"

The Beginning

When Ginger was a small puppy, she had only been weaned from her mother for a short time when she went to live with her human family. She was a beautiful blonde Cocker Spaniel and was an extraordinarily active, smart and pleasant animal. Almost instantly she won over every member of her human family and seemed to fit in as if she were human also. In a short while she had been taught not to mess indoors, chew the furniture or damage things in the home. She was taught to obey what she was told, well most of the time. From the start she was always alert for the chance to escape from where she was supposed to be. It was always in fun but still the people worried about Ginger getting hurt or stolen from the home.

She was wonderful with the children and played endless hours with them. They could do anything with her and they carried her everywhere. She and the kids were always playing catch or games like tug-of-war or hide-and-go-seek. She had been given an old stray sock that was her favorite toy all of her life. They always used that thing for tug-of-war. To play hide-and-seek she would hide her sock and the kids would look for it. Sometimes she would cover her head and the kids would hide the sock. She thought, "Sometimes I'm glad they don't know I can think, this is more fun." They had less fun that way because she always went right to the sock. She also liked to play with her Frisbee, balls of yarn or the kid's toys, especially the dolls. Once she and the kids were in the back yard playing baseball and there was a dispute over the game. She barked loudly to put a stop to the problem but they ignored her. She grabbed the worst troublemaker by the seat of the pants and took him to the mother. Ginger wondered, "Who in the dickens does this darling child think he is?" The mother had heard the commotion and had been watching from the window. She knew how to deal with a poor sport and the rest of the day was pleasant for all.

Ginger not only won everyone over with her wonderful manner of doing things with people, but she was also far superior at the art of conning them into accommodating her wishes. She really was so slick about it that they thought it was their idea in the first place. Even when she was a small puppy she could steal your heart by doing neat stuff to get your attention, which was part of the same con game. For example, she had learned to roll over or sit up and beg. Another stunt was to lay her muzzle on your knee and give you her extremely doleful look. There was no way for any human to resist that or the way she could moan as if she were about to die unless she got her way. The reader may have been fooled by some of the same stunts, just before a smart-aleck dog sneaked off and laughed!

Sometimes she would visit with some of the neighbor dogs and say things like, "I'm ever so grateful that the people think we can't think." When those things happened she felt ashamed for taking advantage of their naivete or lack of understanding.

The worst thing that could happen to Ginger was for someone to disapprove of her and scold her in a low, gentle voice. She would be crestfallen for the rest of the day. Luckily for her and everyone else that was a very rare occasion.

When she was about a year old and had grown to most of her adult size and weight she had been playing with her sock in the kitchen when one of the kids called for her to play. He said, "Here Ginger...Here Ginger...**Here Ginger!**" When there was no response he said, "Hey Mom, where's Ginger?" They quickly searched the house and yard but there was no Ginger. In a short time the whole family was commandeered for a wholesale dog hunt.

Each person was given an area to search and told to ask, "Have you folks seen Ginger?" Nobody within a mile of the house needed to be told what she looked like. That beautiful and loving Cocker Spaniel was well known and highly adored by all who knew her. Most of the people said they hadn't seen her that day. It was like she wasn't anywhere. The family went from busily looking for her, to serious concern, and on up to panic. The mother went from dread of the dog's fate to panic, then wanting to wring her scrawny neck if she was OK. She made sandwiches so the others could eat and go on looking. Soon it was nearly dinnertime and there still was no dog. What could have happened? If she was hiding, where could she be that kept them from finding her? A search like that should have been a job for Ginger. Meanwhile it was getting late in the day and everyone was looking gloomy. All of a sudden there was a meek sounding whine at the front door and one of the kids said, "Well it's about time! C'mon in Ginger. Mom, our mutt is home and I'm afraid she's perfectly OK." Ironically, they never learned what had happened to the head of the household, but indeed she was totally well. All the dog had to do to avoid being skinned alive was to lick every face and wag her tail until it nearly came out of her sitter. Her punishment turned out to be chasing her Frisbee for the kids. They were all a big happy family again.

The next day Ginger was visiting with a neighbor dog through the yard fence and she said, "You should have seen them yesterday! It was a sight to behold when they were looking everywhere for me. Everywhere except under our own porch!"

The other dog said, "One of these days one of your tricks will backfire on you!"

Over the years the family enjoyed endless pleasures playing with their lovable little cocker. She was always an important part of everything they did. No one could have imagined what would happen to Ginger when the school bus brought the kids home from school. Surely they never would have dreamed of how that little bundle of joy would cope with her daily life from that point on.

Ginger's New World- How Does She Cope?

When they brought Ginger home from the veterinary clinic, it was to be a new life for her. Nobody thought to tell her. One wonders how she learned to manage to do the myriad of things that were a part of her every day on earth. Most of the answers were not long in coming. She had many positive factors on her side and what the vet had said about her spunk was a giant understatement. To people's surprise, each mind-boggling chore was no big deal to her. As a puppy she had been taught to sit up and beg. With her leg missing she simply sat up and begged. She placed her hind foot under the center of her stomach for balance and it was a snap.

Earlier when she learned most of her tricks, the teaching was usually by Show-and-Tell. It had worked well then and the mother planned to use the same idea to help her adjust to being handicapped. Things didn't work out that way. The word handicapped means an encumbrance or physical disadvantage. She was not handicapped and needed no crutches or special training. She could easily do anything she ever had done, and just as well. There was no doubt that she was very proud of what she could do and how well she did it.

The family noticed one thing that seemed to bother Ginger. When she heard the school bus approaching in the morning or the afternoon, she seemed ill at ease and worried. That had been the single most traumatic event in her lifetime, and it stayed with her for the rest of her days. Ginger told the neighbor dogs that, "I'm not afraid of the bus, I'm concerned that the kids are O.K. after their day in school."

The mother and father welcomed every chance to play with Ginger or take her for rides. The little creature loved car rides more than anything known to either one of them. In hot weather she would have given her soul to ride with her head out of the car window in the breeze. When they made a sound with the car keys Ginger was ready to travel and she didn't even think of trying to escape. The beautifully magic words were, "C'mom, Ginger!"

As the years flew by the kids gradually became used to the idea that there were certain things around the home that belonged to Ginger, like her two old throw rugs, the Frisbee, her stray sock and her doggy basket. None of them belonged to any other man or beast. If she could have spoken, she would have said something like, "Please keep your grubby mitts off of my stuff!" She made it quite plain that she didn't like for someone to play with her things or, worse yet, to forget to put them away.

Throughout Ginger's life there were a multitude of things she might have wished that she could say to people. She tried desperately to send them messages but they were happily unaware. When she was little, she probably thought very often that she would like to say things like, "Why do you always treat me like a baby? Why do you think you have to show me something over and over? Do you really think I'm that stupid?" After she was grown, she may have been disgusted with some of the things the kids did, like the dispute over the ball game. Maybe she would have said, "I hope your mom wrings your scrawny neck!" There were also many good times, like when they brought her home from the veterinary clinic or took her for car rides, etc. There may have been a million times that she would have loved to say, "I love you so very much...thanks a million...May I please go along?" Or perhaps, "Mom, the kids have been so wonderful to me today that I wish you could give them some kind of a special treat."

The Greatest Escape

Ginger was well known all of her life as an accomplished escape artist. Many times she vanished from sight or hearing in a matter of seconds. She was injured by the bus while she should have been asleep on her doggy basket. For her last escape, she had been asleep on her doggy basket in the living room and the next morning when the mother called, she didn't respond. After she went to sleep she never awoke. She was still on her basket, but will never answer. She passed away peacefully in her sleep, on top of her old stray sock and her Frisbee.

I can hear Ginger saying, "I love the times I had on earth with the family and I wish I could come back. I miss everyone so terribly and I know they must agonize over my absence."

Parting Thoughts

The reader may wonder why Ginger was such a special kind of dog. Do you suppose there was a reason for that? Maybe she was so wonderfully beautiful because of the nice way she was treated by her people. Don't you suppose animals' behaviors are affected by they way they are treated? It is well established that animals become aggressive if they are abused or kept from moving around freely or deprived of healthful and loving care. At the same time there is no mistaking the pleasure of a dog with its head out of the car window on a hot day. If they are kept in cages or tied out on a tether they surely get in foul moods and may get mean. You can add greatly to your happiness if you get a pet and do all you can to make its life terrific. The creature surely will have added happiness at the same time.

III

FLASH THE FIRE DOG

A Future Fire Dog?

Flash's story begins when he was a young puppy about six months old, looking forward to whatever the future had in store for him. One day his mom was away from her puppies and came upon the beginning of a forest fire. She heard a small child crying and found that it was nearly suffocating from the smoke. She started dragging the child downhill toward a nearby creek where she could cool and comfort it. Flash sensed that she was in trouble and he started tracking her from their nest to the fire. When he saw what was happening he grabbed a pants leg and helped her move the victim to the creek.

Afterwards she taught Flash the basics of fire and emergency rescue. His mother said, "Flash I'm ever so proud of you. Some of the other dogs are looking for pups to train for life saving and emergency search and rescue. If you're interested, I'd be glad to ask them to include you." Flash said, "Sure, that would be swell."

When Flash's mother talked to the dogs who taught the course she said that Flash had superior abilities that would be a great asset to his learning and performing the job. She said, "He knows people's thoughts and can read their body language as easily as some persons can read dog's sign language. The sheep herder at the next place has taught him to count sheep and to respond to body signals. He has advanced senses of sight, taste, smell, hearing and touch, plus the sixth sense to feel dangers or catastrophes. Flash sensed that I was in trouble and tracked me down to be of help. He has superior understanding and reasoning, and can quickly evaluate a situation and plan the best way to solve a problem."

The next morning Flash and some other dogs about his size and age were told to report for training in fire fighting and life saving. Two of the *smart dogs* were waiting for them and began with introductions. The older one said, "I'm in charge here, and everywhere else. I don't have a name, just call me Boss. I teach inspiring other dogs and people, obedience and psychology. I'm the toughest dog you'll ever meet and before any of you challenge me, <u>be sure you're ready</u>." It was no great surprise that no one even uttered a peep. After a moment's pause Boss said, "I'd like for all of you to meet one of your group who has an interesting and valuable story to tell. Flash, will you please tell us about your experience saving lives during a fire?" Flash arose and said, "Thank you, Boss. I guess he means the other day when my mom was rescuing a child from a fire by pulling him toward a body of water. I saw what she was doing and helped her. We moved the child down to a creek where it could be cooled and there was less heat and smoke."

Flash continued, "Afterward mom told me some things to always do. You should squint for better vision in smoke, crouch low and work downwind below the worst heat and smoke. Heat rises taking most of the smoke with it. Work downhill for less fire and smoke and to make moving victims easier. Use natural windbreaks for less exposure to fire and smoke. Cool victims and yourself in bodies of water to reduce burn injuries and prevent further tissue damage. Also get in the water as quickly as you can if your hair is on fire." Boss rose again and said, "Thanks Flash. Mates, he just stole my whole lesson and I'm not one bit angry. In fact I'm quite proud to say that Flash did a great job. I think everyone should go over what he said and remember his lesson. Flash and I are both available to answer your questions. You are not dismissed yet, and now is the time to hash it over and be sure you understand and remember today's lesson from Flash."

Boss continued, "As you know, today's lesson also includes psychology for dogs. You have already had your first lesson in obedience, I'm in charge. Since no one argued the point everyone passed. There is much more to come on the subject. When you were in, "Dogs Con School," you were taught a few basic pointers about *inspiring*, *obedience* and *psychology*. I can't overstress the importance of getting people to see what you know that should be done, while thinking it is **their** idea. You may have noticed that Flash and his mother had no contact with humans, she simply knew what needed to be done and did it."

Boss also said, "In most emergencies we must convey the correct idea to people. We are blessed with the ability to share our thoughts and feelings with humans without using speech like they do. As they would say, we con them. This is how we inspire them to take the proper action. When it comes to our own actions, obedience is vitally important. We don't have the privilege to choose right or wrong in an emergency. We have enough smarts to know the right action and we must see that it happens that way. With that said there is a fly in the ointment, sometimes people fail to see the point of our message. Then we must be prepared to justify what we did or explain why we failed to deliver the message and **convince** those who needed to act. The stakes are high, wrong action or inaction often costs lives. Perhaps people's lives and perhaps dog's lives. In the next phase of your training you will act out your duties in a series of simulated situations. Here's where we have to outdo some of our human friends who aren't smart enough to clap with both hands. This seems like a good time to call it a day for now. I feel that all of you have paid close attention to today's lessons. In the morning you will have the chance to ask questions. Good evening mates."

The next morning they met again for class and the Boss answered a few questions, then asked some questions of his own to be sure the lesson was understood and remembered. When the Boss was satisfied with the progress at that point he said, "We will continue with more basics of your training and later we will act out ways of dealing with some simulated situations."

Boss said, "Folks please pay close attention in class and feel free to ask questions if there is something you don't understand. By far the worst type of emergency we face involves fire. We really must watch our Ps and Qs around fire or we will join the list of victims, besides failing to help those in need. There are several simple ways to cope with our job in a fire. We can squint for better vision in smoke and crouch low, below the worst heat. We can hold our breath to lessen inhaled smoke. Remember heat rises, taking most of the fire and smoke with it. We can avoid more fire and smoke by working downhill, also it is easier to move a victim downhill. When you feel you can't possibly move a victim, put your life on the line and be one of the Dogs With the Right Stuff. You can do miracles if you try. We can also use any natural windbreaks to lessen smoke and heat exposure for both the victim and the rescuer. By cooling the victim and the rescuer in water we can reduce burn injuries and prevent further tissue damage. Also we dogs have to keep our hair from burning, or put it out when it burns." Boss felt that the class should take a break before starting the next project. He said, "Mates let's take a break and resume in half an hour."

After everyone had returned Boss said, "Mates our next lesson will be a practical test of the material we have covered so far. At this point my teacher-dog partner Smoky will take over." The other dog arose and said, "I don't care if you call me Smoky or that other smart-dog or whatever, I am here to teach and you're here to learn." He continued, "Before we begin with any practical tests I'd like to break from tradition and tell you about the time when Boss and I were in training as pups. At this point in our training we were told to see if there were people trapped in a house fire. We didn't know that there had been a similar procedure that same day in the house next door and that the fire was still smoking. Boss and I, with our Blood Hound noses, charged right to the wrong house! Fortunately no people or dogs were hurt or killed in that case and we felt a little embarrassed." After the students had a real hearty laugh over the episode, he continued, "We had to go to the vet for a checkup before continuing class but we were OK so all was well. Our next project was to rescue a child that had broken through the ice on a nearby pond. We didn't know that the child was a lifelike doll, tied in place where it appeared to breathe from an air bubble between the ice and the water. Again we charged right in like storm troopers and broke through the ice also. With our usual sharp skills we panicked and went back to the shore, without the 'child'. If it had been an actual child, it would have been scared nearly to death and needed to be rescued by the *'smart-dogs,'* who were not amused. Again it was fortunate that there were no deaths or injuries."

"In case any of you should become teacher-dogs, you should know that as such, you are responsible for all of the good or bad things that happen to your students. Our teachers should have been aware that the ice was softening due to warming weather and even though it was still thick, it wasn't strong enough to support us. It is of paramount importance to be sure that other beings are not harmed by our acts or failures, in any way or for any reason. Have any of you wondered why Boss and I became teacher-dogs? Do you suppose it was a gentle form of punishment? Was there the hope that others would benefit from our mistakes and experiences? You should also know that teacher-dogs do a great service to their dog communities and enjoy great satisfaction from what they do." Smoky continued, "Next we will go ahead with our practical test project. We are about due for a break so why don't we go to chow and reconvene in an hour and a half?"

When the class resumed Smoky said, "I'm going to escort the class to the scenes of the experiences I described." He paused at each site and described what happened and pointed out the things that could have been improved upon. He said, "Boss and I have improved the way this course is taught and I don't doubt for a second that whoever is next in our job will do likewise." After discussions, questions and answers for over an hour Smoky said, "You folks are the best class I've ever been privileged to work with. You have my congratulations, thanks and best wishes for wherever life takes you. Class dismissed!"

New Role in Community?

Flash and his classmates quickly found that they were looked upon with greater respect and admiration after they had completed their emergency training. Other dogs asked all sorts of questions about what was taught and some even offered to help if the need arose. Flash said, "It's unlikely for that to happen, however in that case it would be for a very critical need, requiring you to put your lives on the line for others, perhaps both humans and dogs." Flash added, "Please remember that each and every one of you already has an important role in your human family, which you must always devote your utmost to. If there is no further discussion, I'm needed by my people. Thank you one and all."

The **Firehouse** Explodes!

The day had began as a humdrum routine of activities for the people who lived in the community. The folks at the coffee shop were talking about the weather and the problems with weeds, bike riders and stray dogs, with their usual lack of reality. The barbers and taxi drivers were offering the solutions to all of the world's problems, also as usual. Suddenly there was an explosion that violently shook the buildings and people loose from their serene place in the world.

In a matter of seconds the Fire Siren was blaring its piercing, shrill message to alert the community of an emergency. This was quickly followed by other sirens and alarms, and total confusion among all of those who were responding. The second floor of the firehouse had collapsed upon the eight firemen inside, the fire fighting equipment and the Emergency Response Center. Some of the firemen and the Emergency Dispatcher who coordinated the 9-1-1 calls needed immediate medical care. Two firemen were in the coffee shop across the street from the firehouse and were able to see the problems on the first floor. One of them called the police department, just before it was flooded with calls, and advised them of the situation.

The police immediately closed all entries and exits to the downtown area, except for emergency vehicles. Then they radioed for ambulances and police from other communities to assist at the firehouse. They also radioed for assistance from other fire departments. One department immediately dispatched a pumper and a ladder truck to the scene, to remain there as long as needed.

Just as the first road block was being established, an SUV ran into another vehicle at an intersection, injuring the occupants of both vehicles. As a policeman on the scene was helping the SUV driver, he discovered the radio transmitter that was used to detonate the explosion. He called for backup to arrest the suspect and arrange for security at the hospital.

Meanwhile, in a most remarkable coincidence, Flash's man of the family was an arson inspector named Tom Watson. He took Flash to the scene to see if the dog could be of help. Flash went right to work and almost instantly he sensed that someone was trapped in a room in the back of the station. Flash was unable to claw his way into the room so he began howling for help with their rescue. Flash thought, "It doesn't seem right for me to ask for help in trying to help others, but that is what must happen." He got his owner's attention, and communicated the need for help with the rescue. Soon all of the fire crew which had been on duty were on the way to the hospital, where they were examined and treated as needed. Flash thought, "I'm afraid someone in that other room no longer needs help." His owner followed him to the emergency call center where they found that the operator's head was crushed beneath a large structural beam, and there was no hope of survival. The owner called Flash back out of the way and radioed for security of a possible murder scene, and homicide detectives.

Within less than two hours, there was good news from the hospital, there were no serious injuries and all eight firemen were being treated and released. They had been covered with explosive residue and debris, also one person's glasses were broken.

As the Arson Investigator began to resume his duties, a TV News team appeared like magic and a reporter said, "Good morning Tom, why do they need an Arson Investigator here?" He responded, "I came here to see if people needed help. I'll have to ask you to leave this area." The reporter said, "You don't have the authority to ask me to leave, and I'm surely staying." The Inspector began losing patience and said, "First of all I am also a duly appointed and sworn Deputy Sheriff, and if you don't leave immediately, I'll arrest you, place you in handcuffs and have you transported to jail. Now what will it be?" The reporter said, "You wouldn't dare, haven't you heard of the freedom of the press?" The result was, "Yes I have, and as Deputy Sheriff, you are under arrest. Please extend your arms." The reporter soon had the chance to report directly from jail, and to enjoy the company of some other inmates.

The First Priority-Restore 9-1-1 Services

Flash was thinking, "I must make my owner aware of the need to get someone to provide

35

temporary 9-1-1 service until the normal facility is back in operation or replaced." His powers worked! The man said to the senior policeman on duty, "I just remembered, we need to get the phone people in here to set up something for handling 9-1-1 calls." In less than an hour the telephone crews arrived with the equipment needed and said, "We're here, where do you want this stuff?" Some people at the police department had already been arranging for space. The police chief drove up just in time to answer the question. He said, "We have made room in the city hall, and there is already a switchboard in place which you probably can use." In another hour the new emergency dispatch center was in service and was operated by someone who had just retired as an emergency dispatcher. Flash thought, "Miracles really never do cease, thank God!"

The Fire Department Goes Back to Work

One of the larger fire stations loaned the use of a second ladder truck and the fire chief borrowed a second pumper from the national guard, along with numerous items of other equipment. The fire department was weak, but back on the job, protecting their area. Meanwhile, a local building contractor donated the use of his demolition crew and equipment to clear out enough debris for an open-sided fire station. They didn't have such luxuries as a computer or a kitchen, but they could do the job without a computer and they could eat in restaurants.

Flash Gets Honored & Becomes a Fire Dog

The firemen had a kennel behind their station for their two search and rescue dogs, and it was unaffected by the blast. Those dogs checked with Flash at the fire station to see if anything else was needed. He let them know there was nothing at that moment, and that the emergency dispatch center was back in service. After they left, the leader said, "We should see that they decide to reward Flash for his outstanding contribution." The other one said, "Yes, and the mayor is the easy one to motivate." The leader said, "We need to contact him soon, there is a council meeting this evening." Luckily they encountered the man as he was leaving his office. It suddenly occurred to him that Tom's dog had been a great help at the fire station. When the mayor addressed the council, he said, "I'd like to suggest that we provide a reward to Tom Watson and his dog Flash for providing outstanding service to the community during an emergency. Their actions at the fire station reflect great credit upon themselves, their department and the community."

As a result Arson Investigator Tom Watson was awarded his second Distinguished Service Medal, accompanied by a Certificate of Meritorious Service for his dog, Flash. The entire affair was duly reported in the local newspaper, on the radio and television. A newsperson in the crowd asked the mayor, "Is Tom Watson's DSM awarded for putting one of our people in jail?" The mayor said, "Yes, are there any more questions?"

Later there was a meeting of the various lead dogs and Flash was appointed to their version of a Search and Rescue Team. The Boss even congratulated Flash in the presence of the group. Flash thanked them and said, "I never would have dreamed I'd have the chance for something this great!" The next morning Tom took Flash to the kennel and said, "Flash, you should be with the Search and Rescue dogs. See if you can help." The dogs who were there had already met Flash and thought highly of him. They said, "Flash, you show great promise and we will be glad to show you the ropes."

The leader said, "Flash, we know quite a bit about the factors considered in your selection for Search and Rescue duty, and we feel that you deserve to share that information. In those types of work you need superior intuition, ability to inspire or motivate and the utmost ability to use psychology. Intuition means immediate knowledge without conscious use of reasoning or instinct. Psychology is the science of human and animal behavior. That is what we use to con people into acting as we wish, while believing it is their idea. We use psychology when someone won't comply with our wishes, we make them <u>delighted</u> to comply.

You showed the best of judgment when you inspired others to help you with a rescue, and to induce others to get the emergency services restored. At the same time you displayed the strongest ability to convey your ideas to others, which is the backbone of our methods. The members felt you are blessed with plenty of those qualities. As an added bonus, you are highly respected both by humans and by dogs. We are sure you will obey and cause others to obey, and you will help others to see the need and means for doing something, as well as the advantage of that action. We welcome you among our group." Flash said, "I am so overwhelmed that all I can think of to say is, thanks from the bottom of my heart."

The leader continued, "There is still one more thing we wish to touch on while we are at it. We want you to work and train with us until you have some experience, and then we hope you will be interested in becoming a teacher-dog. We know that

Perry Charles Dodge

you are already a *smart dog*. The next thing for you
to think about is ways to improve the training given
for emergency search and rescue. Whether you
become a teacher dog or not, the course always can
and should be improved."

Flash said, "Maybe several heads are better than
one or two. When the lesson is being planned,
perhaps a committee approach would lessen the
number of oversights, like when the ice was too
soft." The leader responded, "You're right Flash, I
guess that idea is so simple that the two of us
overlooked it. This evening there is another meeting
of lead dogs and perhaps you should introduce and
explain your idea. We will be present to support you
in any way that might be needed. Before you beat
me to the punch, it is we who should thank you."

That evening in the meeting, the Search and
Rescue team Lead Dog said, "I want to set a new
precedent and nominate a member for the position
of teacher-dog. As we already know, Flash has
clearly demonstrated abilities far beyond what most
of us had at the same point in our development.
Despite the fact that Flash has only begun to
formally train for the position on the job, he
demonstrates the needed skills, besides he's a
natural for the job, and those skills should not go to
waste. Furthermore, Flash has suggested a way to
improve what is taught and how it should be taught.

40

I would like for Flash to offer his suggestion to this group." The Chair-dog said, "Flash I feel we must hear your idea, please take the floor."

Flash arose and said, "Thank you for this chance. Mates, I was asked to find ways to improve the training for Emergency Search and Rescue. There have been times when there were serious risks to our members due to lack of planning for the class. For example, once the two teacher dogs had planned the simulated emergency rescue of a child who had fallen through the ice, but they overlooked a hazard. The weather was getting warm and the ice was plenty thick, but it was too soft. I suggest that several heads may be better than one or two, therefore perhaps such lesson planning should be done by a committee. Mates, I thank you for listening." The Chair-dog dismissed Flash and said, "Please wait outdoors, we must discuss this matter first, then we will let you know what we decide."

While he waited there was loud discussion inside, with strong talk for and against using Flash's idea and promoting him to *teacher dog*. When he was finally called back indoors, he was congratulated by the entire group. Those who had opposed the idea were convinced and the final vote was unanimous. When Flash left the meeting he went straight to his mother's den and told her the good news. She said, "Flash I'm so proud of you that there are no words to express my feelings. I've always known you had all that was needed, now I thank God that the others learned it too. I'm sure you will make all of the rest of us proud also. I love you dearly, Flash."

The next morning Flash visited Boss and Smoky to discuss what would happen next. The Boss said, "Flash, we felt right from the first that you would be one of our group before long. We didn't expect it this soon, but it's not a bit too early. We three should go to the next meeting and suggest that such a committee be established right away. I wish to name you as the Chair dog of the committee." Flash said, "Thanks Boss, I hope I'm ready for that position. I do trust and respect your judgment, so if you say I'm ready, I surely am. Thanks Boss." The boss said, "That's another thing, you should be the new Boss dog."

At the meeting there was strong opposition to Boss's suggestion, but he was unchallenged as the boss, so in the final outcome, Flash was the new Boss Teacher Dog. The old boss's name was, "Spot," so Smoky said to Flash, "Congratulations again Flash. Spot, let's go home."

IV

CREAMPUFF
THE COUGAR DOG

Imagine for a moment what it would be like to have an animal in your family that is loving and playful with children, yet provides an effective means of dealing with cougars. Also, imagine the thrills, humor and awe to be experienced in hunting a cougar with a dog.

Introduction

Creampuff is a Doberman Pinscher and Australian Shepard dog who serves the roles of the family dog and a cougar hunter in the Pacific Northwest. Dobermans came from Germany originally. Doberman means breeder and Pinscher means terrier. They are known as a large dog with a short, dark coat. Australian Sheperds come from Australia and are widely used as sheep dogs because they are very obedient and easily trained. They, like the Doberman, can protect the livestock from almost any kind of predator.

While his name is Creampuff, he is called PUFF for short. Puff has a natural ability to do both of his

43

jobs so well that his people never need to worry about their family's well-being or the safety of their animals.

The people in the story include Buck and Olive Thompson of the Smoky Sage Sheep Ranch near the former town of Crookwheel, Oregon. Their foreman is a lifelong friend named Jake Rand. He and his wife Wanda have worked for Buck about ten years. Also prominent in the story are the neighbors Harvey Shaw and his sons, Amos, Bill and Oliver. Others who provided help and medical care are Sheriff Ace Bell and Doctor Marvin Atwood, who was famous for his skill at giving shots.

Temperament

Puff has a dual personality, one is that of a very gentle, easy-going family dog that is wonderful with children and other animals. The other is a vicious or voracious, brute-like monster with such a menacing demeanor that he instills terror in his foes.

As a family dog he has been forced to accept the family cat as a family member and treat it with kindness. That is no small order because people don't know how awful cats smell to a dog, and dogs naturally have an overpowering animosity toward cats. Their odor is more repulsive than any other scent to a dog, and the dog's natural instinct is to avoid or repel what he feels is a disgusting and sickening creature.

Puff's Superior Senses

Puff's senses are far superior to most dogs, which gives him a great advantage over other animals, including other dogs. His vision is so keen that he sees other creatures before they know he is present. When he is hunting cougars, he can see them while they are concealed in thick brush and in dense fog. His hearing is so sharp that he hears cougar kittens meowing from their dens, for miles away. Some people say, "Puff can hear a bug tip-toeing on cotton." Puff has such a great sense of smell that he can follow a cougar's scent several hours after it was in the area. Puff's abilities add meaning to the term extrasensory perception. Closely related to those abilities are the value of his premonitions or hunches. He can anticipate the next moves of an adversary and quickly make counter moves.

The Cougar

The cougar is a large, tawny or dull yellow quadruped, or four-legged animal. It belongs to the feline or cat family. It is also called a mountain lion or a puma. In an Aesop Fable, a lion went on a hunt with other lions and afterwards divided their spoils by giving one third to himself as king, one third to himself as an individual and one third to whoever should dare to take it. That tale gives a good idea of the sort of enemy our hero, Creampuff, was dealing with.

Cougars are predators, meaning that they live by preying on other animals. They are known for using stealth and ambushing their prey, and for picking on defenseless creatures like lambs or other small animals.

The Ranch Protectors

Puff's human family, Buck Thompson and his wife Olive, live out in the country on a ranch and make a living by raising and marketing wool, mutton and live sheep. Puff is regarded and treated as another member of the family. He enjoys a rapport with the people like no other animal on the place. At times the Thompsons have lots of trouble with the loss of their livestock and when they lose an animal they do their best to put a stop to the problem by the best means available.

The actual culprit is liable to be a coyote or a wolf, and on rare occasions they will be raided by a cougar. They have other hunting dogs that they use to control the coyotes and wolves, but cougars are a much more powerful, vicious and cunning creature. The task of hunting and killing them is an awesome, challenging and life-threatening chore.

The Cougar Raid

As we look in on the scene, Buck was riding on horseback around the perimeter of the ranch and came upon the signs of another raid on the livestock. Buck thought to himself, "I knew it had been too long since we've had any losses." He could see where there had been some sort of a scuffle in the sagebrush next to the property line and something had been dragged under the fence and away into the hills. As he moved closer, he could see that there were <u>cougar</u> tracks on the scene! About the same time his horse took the bridle bit in his mouth and ran for dear life in the other direction.

When Buck came into view of the ranch house, Jake, the hired hand knew that something was seriously wrong or his boss would never mistreat one of his horses in such a manner. Jake had worked for Buck for over ten years and they knew each other as well as they knew themselves. Their mutual trust and respect was a once in a lifetime experience for each of them.

When Buck rode into the barnyard the horse let go of the bit and Buck halted him, dismounted and tied the reins to the hitching post. He turned to Jake and said, "I guess we're in for some excitement today. We have been relieved of a lamb by a cougar, over by the south fence line. I'll call the neighbors and you can start getting stuff together. I'll ask Olive to scare up a meal and some sandwiches, then when our help arrives we can start earning our keep."

The Cougar Hunt

In short order they had eaten and made ready for the hunt. By then the neighbors had arrived. After casual greetings they gathered outdoors without further banter or nonsense. Buck said, "Fellows we'll start out the same as last time. Jake and Oliver are the best shots so they can take the flank positions to keep the cougar from doubling back and getting away. Amos is the best tracker so he will follow the critter and lead the fearless warriors, and the rest of us. Harvey and Bill can take the stands on high ground. I'll make radio checks first off and again when we take our positions. Then we'll only use radio when necessary. That leaves Amos and I to do the hunting, kill the cougar and do the rest of the work. Are there any questions?" Amos said, "How come you forgot to give Puff a job, are you saving him for lunch?" Jake said, "Puff's job is protecting the fearless warriors, so you and I have nothin' to worry about." Harvey said, "Is that because you guys are fearless, or because Puff is protecting you?" Buck said, "Fellows, we're burnin' daylight."

Buck didn't say anything about the fact that Amos was the best qualified for tracking because he had ridden into a tree limb and put his eye out. He was a giant of a man and was famous for being the arm wrestling champion, the best tracker in the country and the one to not challenge in a fight. His brothers, Bill and Oliver, had a tough reputation but they didn't dare cross Amos.

The master plan included hunting on foot, so the horses wouldn't spook and throw their riders, which would jeopardize the hunt. As they started out Buck was saying, "Let's watch our step this time, I don't want to see any......yipes!" He tripped and fell like a tree, making the dust boil.

The others gave him a great round of applause and he forgot to finish what he had been saying. Then to add insult to injury, Buck was leading Puff on a leash and when he stood up and brushed off the dust, Puff was wagging his tail. Puff thought to himself, "We're starting out just like last time, except that Buck fell into the watering trough. I'm glad that Jake is here also."

When they got to the site of the lamb's capture, Amos asked the others to wait for him to pick up the tracks and head out after their quarry. In a moment he stepped through the fence and was on his way. It was quite a spectacle, the one eyed, red headed giant was tracking the cougar and leading his pack of fierce hunters. He looked back and said, "Don't say it!" No one knew what he was talking about, but nothing was said.

For the next half hour Amos led the others at an unrelenting trot through huge sagebrush and mahogany, over a steep hill and into a canyon that was forested with pine, cedar and juniper trees. Harvey and Bill had climbed up on their stands. Jake and Oliver were staying a little way behind Amos, while Buck was in the rear with Puff. Puff thought, "Amos seems to think he is tracking a cougar, but I wonder if that one has a mate? If it wanted the lamb for itself, wouldn't it eat the lamb on the spot?"

The excitement was building like a crescendo among all creatures present. Amos could feel in his bones that the killer cougar was near at hand. Puff was straining at his leash and the hair was standing up on his neck like lightning was going to strike in less than a second! People's nerves were tense as a fiddle string and despite the fast pace, no one even breathed! Puff thought, "That varmint is darn close! I can feel it in my shaking bones!"

Back at the ranch house, Olive and Jake's wife Wanda had been talking about the hunts through the years. Olive said, "I've always dreaded cougar hunts the most. You never know what they might do and there is a real problem if they get the surprise on you. I have a terrible feeling that this might be the time we've always feared." Wanda said, "Please get that foolishness out of your head, Mrs. Thompson. If it gets nasty, we know that every man can be counted on for whatever is needed, also don't forget that Creampuff is on the job." Olive said, "Yes, you're right. I'm most grateful that you're with me today. Please call me Olive."

The hunters were inching along slowly now with an alert eye on every tree and bush. It was so deathly still that you could almost hear the dog think. Suddenly there was a muffled sound and Buck was face down on the ground with a cougar biting at his head. Puff was still a few steps ahead of Buck and straining on his leash. When the cougar dropped on Buck, Puff got loose and free to move so he lunged at the cougar and knocked it off of Buck and in a heap. That gave the split second needed for Jake to shoot the huge cat. With the best fast shot known to man, the cougar was deader than the proverbial door nail. Everyone was frozen in their tracks for a few moments while the impact of the situation sank into their minds.

Puff attacked the dead cougar where it was laying and tried to kill it again. When he realized he was too late he thought, "Fiddlesticks, I thought sure I had him dead to rights!" But that was the wrong way to put it. Then Puff remembered, "I was following cougar tracks beyond where that one was in the tree. There darned sure is another cougar, probably the mate of this one."

By the time the cougar was still, Jake was checking on Buck. He said, "Amos, Buck is conscious, please start for the house with him and I'll radio Olive to call 911." He further stated, "To avoid confusion, I'm automatically in charge anytime Buck isn't able."

Jake keyed the mike on his radio and said, "Olive this is Jake, please come in." Olive turned to Wanda and said, "My God! Something bad has happened or Buck would be calling!" She pushed the radio **TALK** button and said, "Go ahead." Jake said, "Buck has been hurt, we don't know how bad, but we are on the way in now. Call 911 and we should be at the house in about 10 minutes." Olive said, "Roger." She called 911 and repeated the information she had. The person she spoke to said, "Yes Mam, please stay on the line." As usual he dispatched Fire, Ambulance and the Sheriff.

Jake said, "Harvey, Bill and Oliver, how about taking our gear and the cougar into the corral?" When they got to the fence Harvey started through first and caught his clothing in the barbed wire so thoroughly that he couldn't even move. Bill and Oliver tried to free him and made matters worse. Amos laughed and said, "Get out of the way, you guys are like a monkey playing football!" Amos eased Buck down and grabbed the cougar and tossed it over the fence. Later they learned that it weighed 240 pounds.

Amos picked Buck up again and carried him the remaining quarter of a mile to the house. The, "football players," managed to free Harvey without cutting his clothes off just as Amos got to the house. If the situation were not so serious, it would have been hilarious.

The Emergency

By the time they got Buck to the house his head was covered with blood and his coloring was almost deathly ashen. Olive put a blanket over him and raised his feet to lessen the chance of shock, just as the emergency teams arrived. In a couple of minutes Buck was in the ambulance and on the way to the hospital. The doctor said, "Get him into X-ray and O.R., stat!" Buck's head had several cuts from the cougar's eyeteeth and he had lost a lot of blood, but he was in satisfactory condition. The X-rays showed no fractures so the doctor said, "Let's sew him up." When he was released from Intensive Care he was sent to a room as the others arrived from the ranch. The doctor met them at the entrance and said, "Hello folks, I'm Doctor Marvin Atwood and we just sewed up Mister Thompson's cuts. He is in satisfactory condition and I want to welcome all of you in to visit while he is wide awake." Olive heard Buck's voice and ran to his side. She said, "Honey, I was terrified but now I'm happier than I can remember to see you in good shape. Thank God!" After they had all visited, the doctor came back in the room and said, "Well, Mister Thompson, I'm afraid you will be a guest of the hospital for a few days. Have you had a Tetanus shot in the last 10 years?" Buck said, "Nope Doc, I'm afraid not, and how about calling me Buck?" The doctor said, "OK Buck. While we're at it, wild cougars are well known for carrying Rabies so we are going to give you a series of Rabies shots, just in case." Buck said, "Do what you must but I won't like it, besides if you run across a tame cougar please let me know."

By the time they finished the series of Rabies shots Buck was about to threaten all of the staff with sudden death. They told him the disease is much worse than the shots. Buck said, "I don't know Doc, I think you're killin' me with all of these precautions." The doctor responded, "Buck, the worst is over by far, you'll soon be back home. Then after a few days recuperating you will be as good as new." Buck said, "If I aint, it's the thrashing machine for you!", with a grin.

The next morning a new nurse came in his room and said, "Mister Thompson, my name is Rita, and if you're ready to get up I'll change your sheets and make your bed." Buck said, "Land sakes Lady, you're pretty enough to do whatever you wish with my bed!" She said, "That's good to hear, when a fellow can flirt he's about ready to go home." That afternoon the doctor called Olive and said, "Come and get this guy, he's looking at the nurses." Olive said, "I'll be right there, and thank you."

The day after they put Buck in the hospital Jake had to start running the ranch and he had his hands plenty full. It was time for planting the crops, sheep shearing and fixing fences all at the same time. That was the natural time for more worries to crop up. He called Harvey Shaw and said, "Harvey, I'm in a dandy fix and I need all the help you and your boys can provide." He answered, "We'll be there in an hour, ready for the whole job." When Jake hung up the phone, he made up a list of what he wanted done and stopped for a cup of coffee. When he rinsed his cup, he saw the sheriff coming into the driveway. As was customary, he walked in and said, "Howdy Jake, I hope I can have a few moments of your time." Jake said, "Sure Ace, what do you need?"

The Reports

The sheriff said, "Jake I hate to bother you with such nonsense, but I have to turn in an Incident Report about the cougar raid on the property. I need you to please answer some questions and I'll write it up. Now:

- When did it happen, the date and time? April 1, 10:00 A.M.
- Was any criminal activity involved? No
- Were there any injuries? Yes
- What is an estimate of the dollar loss to the ranch? $1,000.00
- What medical care was needed? Surgery and Hospitalization
- Can you prevent recurrence? No
A-By better security? No
B-With more manpower? No
C-With more training? No
- Do you have any recommendations for improvement? No

The answers given above were Jake's answers and that was that, until the next day.

The News Media

The next morning before 7:00 A.M. a TV News van came into the driveway. Their crew consisted of a reporter, a cameraman, a sound engineer and a technician. The reporter said, "We just got word about the sheriff's report regarding your cougar raid on the property and we'd like to get your side of the story." Jake said, "You have a copy of the sheriff's report, don't you?" The reporter said, "Yes but we'd still like to hear your side." Jake said, "The sheriff has the basic facts, do you need something else?" The man said, "There's no need for us to have a problem with this, all we want is your side of the story." Jake said, "O.K., my boss found that one of his lambs had been attacked and removed by a cougar. We formed a hunting party and killed the cougar. The boss was bitten and went to the doctor for some stitches and shots. He is going to be alright so that's all there is to it."

The man said, "That's fine, but could you give us a little more detail?" Jake said, "I repeat, you have the facts, do you need something else?" The man said again, "We need more details, and I don't want us to have any trouble over it." Jake said, "That's the second time you've made a veiled threat about trouble, it's time for you and your people to see how fast you can leave the property!" The man said, "We'll leave, but you haven't heard the end of this!" Jake said, "You'd best pray I have, now GIT LOST!"

After the dust had cleared from the TV team's departure, Jake got another cup of coffee and made some notes in Buck's journal about the visit from the news people. As he was rinsing his cup, he heard another vehicle coming, it was the newspaper people from Portland. Jake thought to himself, "This is a beautiful kettle of fish! These folks have made a living all of these years without setting eyes on me, why now?"

The remainder of the day Jake was occupied with the same questions and nonsense as he had been with Sheriff Ace Bell and the TV bunch. Jake said, "Why do you need more facts, do you hope for a Pulitzer?" Somehow he retained his composure until the newspaper reporter threatened Jake with trouble unless he cooperated. Jake said, "That's the last straw, I know my rights and you people have one minute to clear out, and don't ever make the mistake of returning. You can't even spell trouble until you cross me."

Jake made some more notes and went to check on the Shaw crew, and their list of gigantic chores. He saw them gathering tools out by the fence so he went out to them and said, "Howdy fellows, how's it going?" Harvey said, "You didn't say where to start and we figured the fence work needed to be done first. We just finished and I'm sure you'll be proud. I suppose we should do the shearing next and do the planting last." Jake said, "That is swell with me. I also didn't tell you that you're on the payroll for as long as we need you, and while you can spare the time. Now I've had a Devil of a day. I'd like to take you guys to town for steaks."

Later when they had finished eating, they were going over the days events and Harvey said, "Jake, we want you to know that we did something right today. We knew that Buck had planned on changing the weak fence posts, so we did the whole job right, clear down to the last staple." Jake said, "I did something right also, I hope. I evicted a TV News crew and a bunch of newspaper reporters from the ranch. There may be repercussions, but it sure felt great at the time."

Amos said, "It's sad that I can't rightly kid Buck about staying in the back of the men where it was safe. Anyhow I was proud of our fierce hunters and their exploits. Dad and Bill even carried their own guns. Maybe you didn't notice but I went on tracking after I had passed the tree where the cougar was hidden. Jake, I was doubly pleased with your fantastic shot at the cougar, also Buck's incredibly wonderful cloud of dust. I mustn't overlook our hero, Creampuff. Like the rest of us, he didn't even know the cougar was still around until it was messing up Buck's lovely hair. Also the way he fearlessly killed the cougar again was a sight to behold! I'll relish those moments until my dying day." Jake said, "How come you forgot Oliver? You should give him due credit for getting your dad tangled up so much worse in the barbed wire that he couldn't even wiggle. At least he and Bill managed to get Harvey freed without cutting all of his clothes off." While they were talking, Puff was in the back of the room listening. He thought, "I wish there were some way I could let them know that there is another cougar."

Jake looked serious and said, "There's something else I should mention. The cougar raid and the hunt could have been a test of all of our metal by the fellow up above. I'm as amused as any of you about Amos's little speech and I'll also cherish those memories always, but I'd like you to know that I feel the utmost pride in the way everyone who was present will fight to the death when the chips are down. Folks you won't see such a group of people again in a lifetime."

Jake made a few more notes in Buck's journal and was almost ready to go home to Wanda when he heard a car in Buck's driveway. When he looked out, he said, "Great Scott, I wasn't ready for this!" Olive was bringing Buck home from the hospital. Buck had been on complete bed rest for several days and he was so weak he nearly had to learn how to walk again. Buck said, "Howdy Jake, thank God you haven't thrown in the towel on this job. It is wonderful to know that you have everything under control." Jake said, "It is and it isn't, the fence fixing is finished, and it is top notch, but we still have the sheep shearing, dipping and planting to tend to. Also, I threw some TV people and some Newspaper folks off of the place. There might be some repercussions and I have good notes in your journal so I can brief you later." Buck said, "I'm tickled pink and we can go into the details later. Now, Olive can you fix us a snack? I'm dying for some non-hospital food."

Olive said, "Buck, why don't we call Wanda and see if she'd like to join us here? We could have a nice visit this evening." He answered, "Sure honey, go ahead." After they had eaten and were relaxed Buck said, "Jake why don't we go over what has happened while I was gone. I'm sure the ladies would enjoy being included." Buck was glad that Jake asked the Shaws to help and put them to work, and that they were already dealing with the shearing and planting. When Jake related the evictions of the

TV crew and the news reporters, Buck laughed until his sides hurt. Jake said, "It may still come back to haunt us but I sure had my day at the time." Wanda said, "Things like that are why I dearly love Jake. He will die for what's right." Buck said, "I guess I'd better call the attorney tomorrow and brief him in case those hot shots want to cause trouble."

The next morning the Shaws were at the Smoky Sage Sheep Ranch before 7:00 A.M., chomping at the bit to go to work. Everyone had forgotten that someone had backed over the sheep dipping vat with the tractor, and the shearing machine never had been sent to the equipment repair place after it wound up in the barnyard last Halloween. The vat was kindling and the shearing rig was all rusted and had laid in a manure pile all winter. Harvey said, "Jake, just what are we going to do?" Jake said, "Don't sell your sons short. We can stay out of their way and they will have that stuff ready for work in no time." Among the Shaw boys, Amos was in charge, with no questions asked. He said, "Lets get that stuff out where we can look it over, then we can tell what we need." Jake said, "Let us know if you need anything, otherwise we'll stay out of your way. If it's better to buy new gear, we will." Amos said, "Thanks Jake, we'll do what is best."

After they cleaned and inspected the items, Amos told Jake, "Here's a list of what we will need to build a new vat, and I think it will be better to get new shears. I believe we will be shearing tomorrow and maybe do the sheep dipping." All three Shaw boys were top notch mechanics, and while they were waiting for supplies they took the shearing machine apart and had it cleaned and oiled, except for the shears. When the supplies arrived, they changed the shears on all three shearing heads, and built a new vat. By 4:00 P.M. everything was in like-new condition and Amos said, "We can play for about an hour, tomorrow we shear and dip. The next day we inspect the grain drill, and maybe plant Buck's Federation Wheat." Jake said, "I'd like for you three to please join us at Buck's house next."

Back at the house Buck asked Jake how things were going and Jake said, "Quite well, I've got to finish up and I'll join all of you." Jake told the rest, "Unless someone has a darned good reason otherwise, let's all have supper in town on good old Jake!" There were no objections and as soon as they were presentable, they were on the way to town.

In the restaurant, when they were ready to order Jake said, "I won't dictate what people eat this time, the last time I made the Shaws eat steaks. Order what you like, and don't forget that I'm buying." When all eight had finished eating and were drinking extra coffee, Jake said, "Now is a good time to bring everyone up to date on our whole operation. First of all I was tickled pink to see Buck back home and he sounded pleased that I hadn't quit. Buck and I dropped the ball by forgetting that the shearing machine and the sheep dipping vat were out of commission. Amos, Oliver and Bill performed a miracle by rebuilding the shearing machine and building a new vat in about five hours. The equipment is in like new condition. They deserve a round of applause." They were amply applauded. "Amos says they plan to shear and dip tomorrow. I think they are aiming too high, but I'll be helping so maybe we can. The next project is to get the grain drill checked over and operating, then do the planting. I figure five days to plant almost a quarter-section. Any questions?" When there were no questions Buck said, "The hardest thing for me to do is to do nothing and stay out of everyone's way. I've estimated that Amos, Oliver and Bill saved me close to two-thousand dollars on the equipment they repaired and I hope to make it fair on payday. Olive says I'm not to even think about the ranch for a few more days, and I know I can do that with you folks on my team. Thanks again to one and all." Jake said, "Tomorrow will be here soon, maybe we should call it a day, and thanks again from me also."

Next the Shearing, dipping and Planting...Unless?

Amos said, "I've been troubled about our hunt every since it happened. As I mentioned, both Puff and I went on past the cougar and went on tracking. I can't accept the idea that Puff and I were both wrong. The only way it makes sense is if there is another cougar. Now I'm torn between cougar hunting tomorrow or doing the other things first. Jake, I'd like to hear your input." Jake said, "Good grief, I never even gave that idea a thought, but now I feel sure you're right!" Jake added, "Buck, I feel our only move is to go hunting in the morning. The rest can wait a few days if need be." Buck said, "Maybe we're all as dumb as we were about the equipment that needed repair. If there's no known reason not to, we'll be after cougars in the morning." Olive said, "We?" Buck said, "I guess I'll help keep the home fires burning." Puff thought, "My prayers are answered. It's too bad that Buck can't provide the entertainment."

Another Cougar!

The next morning there was no delay in setting about the task at hand. Jake said, "We're short one hand so we'll have Amos tracking, Oliver and I on the flanks, Harvey will lead Puff, and Bill, you can be in back of your dad. Our procedures will be the same, except I won't fall in the watering trough or in the dirt, that's Buck's job. Let's take a moment to check our gear and the radios, then we have to get to work."

They went beyond the tree the cougar had hidden in and began where they had left off. Amos had to circle his last position a few times to pick up the tracks again, then he resumed his steady trot through the brushy and forested terrain. Puff was climbing a steep hillside behind Amos and poor Harvey was gasping for breath. Then the wind changed and Puff suddenly got a whiff of some very fresh scent! He strained on the leash so hard that Harvey nearly lost his grip on the leash. Harvey said, "Hold it, folks. Jake, can someone else take the dog? I'm about to lose him!" Jake said, "Sure Harv, Bill please trade with your dad." Then Amos thought he heard an unusual noise and paused to listen. There wasn't a sound. Puff whined and pulled Bill over the top of the hill like he was a small child. For a few moments more Puff went along easily on the leash. Then the wind changed again and Puff pulled for all of his might and whined again! Amos said, "Both times Puff has been excited, the wind has been from our left. Puff is letting us know that's the way to our cougar!"

Amos had only gone a few more steps when the cougar's trail turned straight to their left. They had dropped down into a shallow canyon and began to climb again. Amos motioned for the others to be quiet and slowly eased along. It was so quiet it seemed like you could hear the grass growing. Then Puff thought, "What was that moving up on the cliff?" He strained at his leash again but he didn't see anything more.

Jake thought he sensed motion at the same time and he tensed, waiting for a target to appear. He thought, "I'm sure glad I remembered my rifle and some shells, we are close to a cougar. Then Puff thought, "I'm sure I heard a cougar kitten! I think there is a mother and some kittens in a cave somewhere up that cliff. The time is about now!"

Buck said to Olive and Wanda, "I'm going crazy with this waiting, I'm sure they are on the trail of something or they would have been on the radio by now. I feel about as valuable as a hog with a sidesaddle!" Olive said, "Honey, you are worth even more than that. Don't forget you have the services of Puff and his assistants. They may have to grind the cougar up with a food chopper so they can bring it out." Buck said, "I desperately need food, coffee and a snort of good whiskey. I'll gladly settle for the fresh coffee." Wanda said, "I just put a pot on to percolate, it will be ready in about five minutes."

The tension eased a bit in the house and they went back to being patient.

Jake was intently watching the cave entrance where he had seen motion when the clouds parted from over the sun and he couldn't see a thing! He thought, "Of all of the rotten luck!" Meanwhile Oliver saw the image of a huge cat on a ledge beside the cave. He thought it was about three hundred yards and quite a challenge of a shot, but he probably wouldn't have another chance so he took a steady aim and fired. The cougar fell like a pole-axed steer and laid still. Oliver yelled, "I got 'im!" Jake said, "Don't be too sure, they have nine lives." Oliver said, "I'm sorry you didn't get the chance Jake, but that was his last life."

Amos scaled the cliff up to the ledge where the dead cougar was and said, "Oops Jake, I got **her**! She is as dead as the, 'Double-Dead Maiden', of literary fame." By that time Bill had led Puff up to the cave and he found the cougar's baby kittens asleep in their nest. Puff thought, "It's a shame that they have such a horrible smell because they are so cute that I'd love to find a way to save their lives." Then Bill was at the entrance and when his eyes were accustomed to the dim light he said, "I'm going to take these little critters to the house. There must be a way for them to be cared for and raised as cats." Amos said, "I'll give you a hand, there's too many for one person. Besides the other men need to learn about the pleasures of carrying that big cat in from here." Puff thought, "I'm thrilled that those guys have enough of the right stuff to tend to those little tykes. There is some justice in the world."

Jake yelled up to Oliver and Bill and said, "What's going on up there?" Oliver answered, "We're carrying out eight kittens and the mother is waiting for transportation to the ranch." Jake pushed the TALK button on his radio and said, "Olive or Buck, this is Jake, please come in." Buck responded and said, "Is everyone O.K.?" Jake said, "We've never been better, partner! We're bringin' in eight live cats and one dead cat. We should be there in about two or three hours. Meanwhile you may want to call Animal Control and see if they can provide for the care of eight tiny, cuddly and beautiful cougar kittens." Buck said, "Roger, by the time you get in, maybe you can struggle your way through a hot meal." Jake added, "Please don't call 9-1-1, I've had about enough reporting to do me. Bill and Amos are coming in now with our gear, plus Puff and the kittens." Buck said, "You're the boss Jake." Puff thought, "I don't see how it can get any better than this!"

On about the tenth ring a man's voice said, "Animal Control, John speaking." Olive said, "This is Olive Thompson from the Smoky Sage Sheep

Ranch, near the small town of Crookwheel. We just
killed a predatory cougar and it was a female with
eight kittens. We want to know if there is some way
that the kittens can be saved and turned over to,
perhaps a zoo or wildlife exhibit for the public to
enjoy?" He responded, "I don't know, I suppose so.
When can you bring them in?" Olive asked, "Is
there someone there who can answer my
questions?" He said, "I don't know, I suppose
maybe our Director might be able to." She said,
"May I speak to him?" He said, "I don't know, I
suppose you can. I'll check, please hold." Olive was
about to the end of her patience when another man's
voice said, "Hello Mrs. Thompson, this is Bill
Temple, the Director of Animal Control. How may I
help you?" Olive repeated her message and added,
"I'm pleased that I am not speaking to another
person like that man named John. Mainly he must
not know anything, and besides he must not have a
last name. Maybe they never found out who the
poor fellow's father was." Mr. Temple assured her
that she would never have to deal with that person
again. He also said, "Mrs. Thompson, I know the
kittens can be donated to either the Washington Park
Zoo in Portland, or the Wildlife Safari in Roseburg.
Also, you won't have to bring them to Animal
Control. We will gladly pick them up, have the
Veterinarian make sure they are healthy, and deliver

them to whichever place you choose." Olive said, "I know I'd rather see them go to the Wildlife Safari. Mr. Temple, I'm thrilled with your way of dealing with me and the needs of those little babies. I don't know how I can thank you enough. THANKS!" He then said, "It's me who should thank you for caring about nature. By the way, if you wish we can also dispose of the dead cougar." She said, "That would be great and thanks again."

Three of the fearless hunters were struggling to move the dead cougar to the ranch and things were not going particularly well. The carcass had easily slid downhill from the ledge to the bottom of the shallow canyon, but it didn't wish to continue. Jake said, "If we use our heads, there must be a harder way to handle this critter." They were soon to learn that this one also weighed two hundred and forty pounds. It was too much for one of them and too awkward for two or three, who were Jake, Harvey and Oliver. Jake said, "Maybe we can tie her pairs of feet together and shove a pole through so two of us can carry the ends of the pole on our shoulder. Let me show you what I mean." Oliver said, "I brought some nylon cord that should do the trick." When they got to the top of the first hill, Harvey said, "I sure miss Amos. I guess I never knew what a man he is. Do you remember how easily he carried the other cougar?" Jake said, "Yep." Then they stopped to rest and Oliver sat on the cougar. He said, "I sure hope the big ones don't decide to check on this one. Amos and Bill have our guns. Maybe we should go cut us a switch."

When they got the cougar to the place where they crossed the fence they stopped for another break. Then after a few moments they began working the cougar under the wires and then climbed through, except for Harvey that is. He snagged his clothes in the barbed wire, again. Oliver tried to free him and got him so tangled that he couldn't move, again. Jake said, "I've lived nearly two-hundred years and I've never seen anything like this!" Then they noticed Puff standing a few yards from them, wagging his tail and watching. Puff thought, "I'm a little shy of two-hundred years, but I sure agree. I'll drop by in the morning and see how they're doing." Puff calmly went back to the house.

Finally the big occasion arrived, they got the cougar to the barnyard. When they went inside Jake looked Amos in his one eye and said, "Don't even say a word!" After they had eaten some of the finest Prime Rib Roast Beef in the world, they were a lot more sociable and the latest great feats of the fearless hunters were discussed. Jake forgot to mention the second mishap with the fence, but Oliver made a big production of it. He finished with, "Jake said he had lived nearly two-hundred years and he has never seen anything like this." Buck laughed until his headache returned and Jake said, "That serves you right, Buck."

Jake poured another cup of coffee and made the usual entries in Buck's journal then said, "Well fellows, the vacation is over, here's what's next. Tomorrow this bunch of overworked ranch dogs will have to do a little bit of work. If we hope to shear and dip two-thousand head of sheep before summer and winter are over, we'll need all of the help we can get."

The next morning the crew was still without Buck, but they had the help of five dogs. It was an unbelievable sight to see when Jake started to tell Puff what he needed and the other dogs did as Puff somehow directed. Jake called, "Puff, get them in the barnyard." Jake opened the gate and the other dogs gathered the sheep and headed them into the coral, then Jake closed the gate. Jake said, "Keep one sheep by each chute while we work." Puff never moved and there was no visible sign that he gave them any message, but the other dogs did exactly as Jake wished.

Next the Shearing and Dipping...The Second Attempt

The shearing shed was a long covered pen with no walls and it had chutes to route the sheep into pens with shearing machines. Then the sheep went to the dipping vat for a bath in sheep dip, or crude oil, to kill lice, ticks and other insects in their wool. The open building kept the sun and rain off of the workers and animals. The process of shearing the sheep was an advanced art in itself. Jake told the others, "Here's the easiest and fastest way to position and shear a sheep without skinning it or working yourself to death." Jake demonstrated exactly how each step of the shearing and dipping was to be done. Then Jake said, "Puff, keep one sheep by each chute, and move them to the field after they leave here." Jake pointed to the place he was talking about as he spoke. He said, "Here's where you will find out how valuable Creampuff really is. Lastly, we will take a five minute break and play musical chair with our jobs each hour. Let's get to work!" Right from the start, Puff was pleased at the way the other dogs were smart enough to do their part in keeping things working as Jake wished. Puff thought, "We're surely blessed with these mongrel mutts."

As the crew worked, Buck said, "Olive, have you and Wanda noticed how smoothly they are running that whole operation? I can't imagine how they have managed to use the dogs for moving the sheep, but I can see that they are. I fondly admire each man and dog." Just then three trucks turned into the driveway and Buck could see the vehicle door signs that read, "Baker County Animal Control." When they got out of their trucks, they showed good judgment in not disturbing the shearing and dipping. They went on in the house and the leader said, "Hello folks, I'm Bill Temple from Animal Control." He turned toward Buck and said, "Are you the guy to deal with?" Buck said, "Yep, I'm Buck Thompson. I'm your man and I welcome you folks to our place. What can I do for you, Mr. Temple?" The response was, "Please call me Bill, and I guess the question should be what can we do for you about the cougars?" Buck said, "Likewise, you can call me Buck. If you folks can spare the time, we're about ready for the noon meal and after we all polish off our heaping plates I'd love to show off our miracle dog, 'Creampuff the Cougar Dog' who has started running the whole place."

Jake and his crew came in just then, and they had cleaned up for lunch before coming in the house. After introductions were made all around, they gave serious attention to Olive and Wanda's normal efforts in the kitchen, which were unsurpassed. After the meal Buck said, "Jake, would you mind taking the time to relate our two cougar hunts and show all of us how you and Puff control the shearing and dipping?" Jake said, "Nope, I can't spare the time." He continued by briefly relating the details and prompting continued laughter. "If all of you will follow me, I'll show-and-tell how Puff runs the show. We call Creampuff, PUFF." Jake only took about ten minutes to vividly relate the hunts and show off their handiwork with the sheep. Then he said, "Puff, lets get back to work."

Buck, Olive, Wanda and the Animal Control people gazed in awe for a few minutes as Jake's men and Puff's dogs continued the assembly line like operation with the sheep. Then Bill Temple said, "I wish to express our appreciation for everything, especially the food, entertainment and education." Olive said, "I made a nest for the little cats in a cardboard box which you may wish to use to move them, or perhaps you have pet carriers of your own." Bill said, "Thank you, Olive, but we are equipped to handle both the live kittens and the deceased mother. Provided the kittens are O.K., they will be on the way to Roseburg and the Wildlife Safari tomorrow. We'll be out of your hair in a few moments. Thanks again for the wonderful meal and your gracious hospitality." Olive replied, "What can

I say, you're always more than welcome." In less than five minutes the cougars were on the way to their respective destinations and Buck returned to his routine of supervising nothing. He thought, "Now I'm twice as thankful for each person and each dog. We are truly blessed."

After the sheep shearing and dipping had resumed, Buck, Olive and Wanda had been relaxing and talking during the free time the ladies had before beginning to fix the next meal. Wanda had been admiring the Thompson home with it's expertly crafted woodwork and it's unusual comfort and convenience. She had remarked, "I'd give all three teeth for a place like this."

In the shearing shed, the crew was getting well accustomed to the routine of rotating jobs and sending about two or three sheep a minute out for the dogs to herd back to the field. It was Oliver's turn to put the sheep in the vat, and it was not to their liking. The older ones had been dipped before and knew the smell of the crude oil used in the process. Suddenly a sheep nearly got loose and threw Oliver off balance. KERSPLASH, Oliver fell in the vat! He even got crude oil in his eyes and he howled like a stuck pig! Amos was nearby and quickly helped him out, then said, "Oh my, you poor little fellow, I didn't know you were ready to get deloused. Just look at your hair. You had better clean up, and don't forget to wash behind your ears." Then the whole crew was in total pandemonium, the dogs were barking and the sheep were scattered all over. Jake figured to himself, "Well, here's another day shot to the Devil!" By then the others were out of the house and the shed, "helping," Oliver. Jake said, "It's only about a half-hour until supper anyhow. We'll shut her down and go like the dickens tomorrow. It looks like we've done a little over half of them."

Oliver tactfully but determinedly refused to clean up at the Thompson place. He said, "If you have an old dog blanket or something I can use on the pickup seat, I'll clean up at the house." Soon he was back, nearly as good as new and adequately starved. When they finished eating, Olive said, "I hope you folks have saved room for chocolate cake and ice cream." When they had finished, there was little time wasted visiting before the whole crew went to bed. They were dog-tired.

The next day the shearing and dipping continued without interruption until lunchtime and the waiting herd was growing smaller. When they had finished eating, Jake said, "Buck I'm getting worried. It scares me when things go so darned smoothly. At our present rate we'll finish the sheep this afternoon. Since Oliver got oiled there's no stopping the whole crew." Buck said, "It seems to help a lot for me to stay out of the way. I've been thinking about turning the Smoky Sage Sheep Ranch over to you and Mister Creampuff." Amos said, "That may not be too smart, Puff didn't even help poor Oliver out of the vat." Oliver said, "I've heard about enough, 'poor Oliver', for the present." Then Jake said, "We're burnin' daylight, let's finish the sheep."

After the sheep were being processed again, Olive said, "Buck why don't we go to the doctor this afternoon and see when you can resume some of your activities?" Buck said, "Swell, Wanda would you mind staying while they're working in case they need something?" Wanda replied, "BUDDY-YOU-GOT-IT!"

Free at Last!

Doctor Atwood checked Buck over thoroughly and said, "Well Buck, this is the day you've been waiting for. You're released from my care and I suggest you be careful and go back to your job gradually. I know that those Rabies series are a tough ordeal, but at least you're immune to Rabies for life. By the way, the cougar was not Rabid." Buck said, "Thanks doc, that's sure a great comfort." Olive said, "Doctor Atwood, I want you to know that we are thankful beyond words, and Buck didn't mean to sound sarcastic."

When Buck and Olive got back to the ranch, Puff's crew of dogs were herding the last of the sheep out to the field. Puff let the other dogs know that he was very proud of the way they performed every move. They knew that he thought, "I never realized that every one of you are worth your weight in gold. I only wish I could let the people know how we all feel about them. Now I feel sorry that you didn't get to be in on the cougar hunt. Maybe it's just as well, one of you might have been hurt. We sure have had some great laughs at some of the dumb stunts our people did for our entertainment. I'll always remember Buck's dust cloud and his messy hair, Harvey's being caught in the fence, the time all of us were unaware of the second cougar, the cute little kittens and last but not least, Oliver's new hair oil." The dogs were relieved that they could finally think about something besides the sheep.

It was mid-afternoon when they finished with the sheep, but they had to clean up and store all of the equipment so it was almost suppertime when they washed up and went into the Thompson home. Buck, Olive and Wanda were both relieved and thankful that the sheep were finally cared for and ready for the rest of the season. Jake said, "We've been mighty lucky so far. I don't want to sound ungrateful, but I'll rest easy when one more small chore is done. Tomorrow is the day for planting. In the morning we will check the grain drill over and make sure it is ready for its job, then we have to work." Puff had been listening in the background and he thought, "What the heck is a 'grain drill', I've never heard of such a thing?"

Planting the Federation Wheat

The next morning Jake said, "Why don't the rest of you guys look over the grain drill? I want to talk over a couple of things with Buck while I have the chance." Amos said, "Sure Jake, let's hit it fellows," and they were on the way out. Jake said, "Buck I've been wondering, 'Why do you seem to be holding back on planting your Federation Wheat?'" Buck said, "I've been reluctant because it's supposed to be a real hard wheat and it should be grown in very cold weather. I think it's been too warm." Jake said, "I know that, but they are growing that stuff down in Texas and New Mexico, with great success. It isn't as hard, but it is healthy and the kernels are larger. I'd like for us to give it a try." Buck said, "In over ten years I've never been hurt by your judgment, so hop to it, Jake!" Puff was thinking, "This has got to be good! I can't wait to see what wonderful entertainment is in store for us this time." Buck said, "You mentioned that you'd like to talk about a couple of things. What else is on your mind?" Jake said, "I have been so pleased with the way the Shaws have done on the job that I thought you might be smart to use one or more of them in your operation. It's something for you to think about." Buck said, "I will think about it, you surely are right about their being hard to beat."

Jake went out and joined the others and said, "How's it look? Are we ready to plant some wheat?" Oliver answered and said, "Yep, we sure are." They had already made sure everything was properly serviced, and the drill hoppers were loaded. They were hooking the tractor to the drill and Amos said, "Let 'er rip!" They had drawn straws and Bill was the first to drive the tractor, so he was finishing the first round when the tractor quit, stone dead. Jake said, "Well, what in the Sam-Hill is it this time?" In moments the crew of master mechanics were troubleshooting the problem. Amos said, "Jake, we aint gittin' no ignition!" Jake said, "Hold on while I get my ohmmeter out of the pickup. I'll see if it's wiring." Jake and Amos checked all of the wires and found nothing wrong. Amos said, "Let's see if the magneto is rotating." They checked it and it wasn't. Then they removed the "Mag" to see if the shaft was sheared. It was. Jake said, "It's break time, while we see about getting a new Mag."

Jake told Buck, "We're in the market for a Mag for the tractor, the shaft is sheared." Buck said, "Help yourself to the phone." Jake called repair shops in Baker, Bend and Pendleton with no luck. He took a deep breath and called Portland. They said, "Sir, we have two on the shelf." Jake said, "I'll take half of them. How about sending it by express?" When Jake got off of the phone he said, "Buck, I've got a new Mag on the way from Portland and we'll have it in the morning. It doesn't even cost as much as a new tractor." Buck said, "That's fine Jake, you're doing the best you can and we have to have it." In the background Puff was thinking, "I wish I hadn't been waiting for more humorous mishaps. These folks sure deserve a decent break. If I have my way the rest of the job will go O.K., and I usually get my way." Later Puff was thinking, "I let the dogs know how highly I valued their help with the sheep, but I wish I had a way to clearly let the people know how proud I am of the way they do things. We dogs are a bunch of lucky dogs."

As usual, Puff had his way. The rest of the planting was finished with no other holdups and the grain crop developed into the most bountiful they had ever grown, with a yield of over a hundred bushels to the acre, and of the highest quality. Puff thought, "My prayers have been answered again!

Now I've got to atone for hating the cat and mistreating it. It can't keep from smelling the way it does."

When the crew finished the planting and stored the equipment Buck said he wanted them to have a good old-fashioned barbecue to celebrate the occasion. The next afternoon after they had all stuffed until they were uncomfortable Buck said, "I have a few surprises for all of you. First of all I happened to learn something that wasn't made public about our recent helpers, the Shaws. Harvey, I know that you and your sons are about to be out of a place to live. I want to talk to the four of you about some kind of a deal for joining the Smoky Sage Sheep Ranch. Think it over and be ready to say your piece, but not until you hear what's next. Now, Jake and Wanda, I want you to think about being the owners of the ranch. I am now able to give you just about any kind of deal you want. By the way Jake, Wanda recently remarked that she would give all three teeth for this home. Olive, you've been wanting for us to get a motor home and travel, if I get to make up for a few years with no fishing, we're ready." Harvey said, "If any of you boys have any objection to us living and working here, please speak up now. Otherwise I hope Jake and Wanda take over here and the Shaw bunch can live at their present Rand place. We surely can work either for

Jake or Buck." Amos said, "I might have to crack a skull or two, but there are no objections." Buck said, "You Shaws will find checks under your dishes, with my thanks." Amos said, "Holy cow! I've never seen $5,000 before!"

Things started falling into place and inside of a week the whole deal was closed. Soon the Thompsons were on a prolonged fishing trip, the Rands owned the Smoky Sage Sheep Ranch, and the Shaws lived where the Rands had been. A lot of improvements were being made all over the ranch. Things were well organized and efficient under the control of the new foreman, Amos Shaw.

There no longer was, "Puff and his dogs," they were equal and respected alike by humans and dogs. Puff let the rest of the dog family know that he was thinking, "We are all a family. If anybody or anything tries to go against any of us, they have our whole bunch to deal with. For a long time I regarded the rest of you as a bunch of Mongrel Mutts. I was wrong and I apologize for that."

None of them heard of Buck and Olive for about two months, then one day they came in the house with a large ice chest full of fish as a gift. It was a quiet day and the Shaws joined them for lunch and a few hours visiting. Harvey said, "I nearly forgot to say, I'm going to be married again and I strongly wish for all of you to be at my wedding." Jake said,

"I never knew if you ever were married. Amos said, "Our mom died from cancer about ten years ago. We know dad's new lady and we wholeheartedly approve." Wanda said, "You can bet your life we'll be there."

V

THE GOLD MINE DOGS

This is about the family dogs around a gold mine and their adventures learning about nature in the wilds. The writer uses wisdom and humor to show how the people in the story coped with their daily trials and tribulations. Also the thoughts and feelings of the dogs are expressed as we humans would speak or write. The story setting is in eastern Oregon and spans the time frame from the early 1930s until the mid 1940s.

Introduction

Patches was a wonderful black and white spotted Fox Terrier. He was brave, adventurous, pleasant and loyal to his friends, who were his human family, the Watermans, and his constant companion, a dog named Gerry.

Gerry was a tan and brown Airedale Terrier who was happy when he was playing with his human family or Patches, or lying in the sun, or laughing at Patches.

How can dogs laugh? Maybe you can't hear it, but they can. You can tell by their actions and expressions when they are mad, glad, sad or in just about any mood. Patches and Gerry would bow down with their paws spread flat when they wanted to play and often they would wag their tails. They were especially happy when riding in a car on a hot day with their head out of the window. They can let you know if you are about to be bitten or if they are ready for a dog fight. They can bare their teeth and snarl so that you have no doubt, yet most dogs love to go for a walk with their human friends. Nearly everyone has heard that the dog is man's best friend but you must experience for yourself the joys of their companionship and love. Dogs feel love, hate, fear and the other emotions experienced by humans. When they lick your face, they probably want food, water or companionship. Dogs have no objections to doing whatever their people wish for them to do, regardless of how silly, difficult or how they happen to feel at the time.

Teaching Patches About Gold Mining

Patches and Gerry had an exciting life, their human family owned and operated a gold mine. Gerry was older so he taught Patches about the mines. Gerry said, "Pay attention and I'll teach you what I know about mining. Let me know when there's something you don't understand." We humans don't know how, but dogs do *talk* somehow. They do manage to communicate with each other.

Patches and Gerry always seemed to be deeply engrossed with the daily activities in the mines. They stayed right in the middle of everything and it seemed like they dreaded the thought that they might miss something, just like two mischievous kids. Their people's hair quickly turned gray from worrying about the dogs' well-being.

Gerry began explaining the mines and mining to his friend Patches. "A gold mine is a place where people look for gold in the earth. Near the surface are dirt and debris, which are washed away with water down to bedrock or layers of hard rock. This method of mining is called Placer Mining by the people. That and Hard Rock Mining will soon be explained." But first Patches was getting tired and bored. Gerry understood and took him back to the house where there was always fresh food and water. After he had one of Grandma's fresh, hot buttered biscuits, he was ready for a nap. When he awoke, Grandma gave him another biscuit just as they heard a strange car coming up the hill near the house. Patches started running and trying to bark with the biscuit in his mouth. It sounded so funny that Grandma laughed and Gerry howled until both of their sides hurt.

That evening Gerry told Patches, "There is lots to do for fun in the mines, but first there is much more you need to learn." Patches always liked fun so he was all ears. Gerry continued, "Placer mining uses lots of water to wash away the loose materials and expose the gold. The gold doesn't wash away also because it is many times heavier than water." (A pint of pure gold weighs 19.3 pounds whereas a pint of water weighs 1 pound). Gerry said, "People use a thing called a *Giant* to wash away the loose materials. It gives a very powerful stream of water, much like a fire hose. They generally start a new mining pit by cutting the earth down to bedrock with the Giant first, then widening out a work area and finally undercutting one side of the pit until the dirt bank cracks loose and caves in. The two most important things you must learn are to avoid being hurt by the stream of water from the Giant or the falling dirt bank during a cave-in."

Patches was in his glory when the bank began to crack. He would stand next to the crack and when it widened enough, he would drop down in the crack and land on top of the dirt when it tipped outward and fell to the bottom of the pit. He would yell, "Yowweee," on the way down. Patches knew how to avoid being hurt by the water from the Giant and there was no mistaking the smile on his face. He did it hundreds of times and had a ball while everyone else panicked each time. Gerry tried it a time or two, but soon seemed to lose interest. He said, "Rats, I'm getting too old for such nonsense!"

Patches also liked to bite at the high pressure, high velocity stream of water from the Giant but it pushed him away and seemed to hurt his mouth. Gerry wasn't interested in that dumb stunt either, he'd rather lie in the sun and scowl at Patches. Sometimes he got disgusted with Patches' stupid-darned-fool antics. Once he said, "We're sure going to miss you around here, Patches. The only way you might avoid being badly hurt or maybe killed in the mines would be if you're struck by lightning!"

Earlier we explained that Placer Mining is washing the loose material away from the gold, and that the gold doesn't wash away also because it is many times heavier than water. Actually they washed the material away with the Giant, which washed out some of the gold also, but it was trapped on the way away from the pit by a *Sluice Box,* which trapped the heavier gold and let the lighter *Tailings* wash away. We also mentioned *Hard Rock Mining,* in which they used blasting powder to loosen bedrock or other material that is too difficult to wash away with water. They had to drill holes in the rock and insert sticks of dynamite in the holes, then detonate it to loosen the rock. Next they moved the loosened material called *ore* to a Stamp Mill, which pulverized the rock, allowing them to separate the rock from the gold and save the gold. Gerry had trouble explaining Placer Mining and Hard Rock Mining to Patches but he kept on trying until Patches understood.

Patches Learns About the Bird Area

Patches loved to explore near the mines. There were many things he could figure out for himself, but some he had to ask Gerry about. Patches had always been interested in animals. Gerry had told him, "Unlike plants, animals can move voluntarily but can't make their own food. Also birds are the only ones who can fly." He further said, "You can tell the birds apart by their sounds and colors." Patches knew the area around the mines very well. The Placer Mine was in a deep canyon called Spanish Gulch. Nearby were Mule Gulch and Sand Gulch. Up the hill between Mule Gulch and Spanish Gulch was an area with lots of birds, called the bird area. One day in the bird area Patches heard a loud, harsh, squawking yell! He froze in his tracks! What was that? Just then with no warning something landed on his back! He turned his head enough to see a black and white mischievous looking bird. It made no move to hurt him but he remembered something Gerry had said, "Don't be afraid, they are only magpies."

Moments later he saw some small birds scurrying for cover and making cooing sounds. He tried to look closer but they flew so suddenly that he was nearly scared out of his wits. They can reach full speed almost instantly and their wings make a terrifying noise. Later, on the way home Patches met an animal about his size with two white stripes on its back. It seemed friendly so Patches bowed down to show that he wanted to play. To his surprise it stood up on its hind legs. Patches waited to see what was next and in a moment it turned and went off in the brush. He wished he had tried to talk to it and perhaps make friends, but the chance was gone so he went home. His only thought was, "Rats, he might have been nice to know."

Patches told Gerry about his adventures when he got home. Gerry said, "You were right about the magpie and the small birds were quail. Magpies are well known for their mischief. They have a loud, harsh yell and like to chatter for food. They aren't harmful but they can be very annoying with pranks like stealing your things. You need to protect your property anyhow." Patches needed to go to the bushes and Gerry asked him to come right back. Patches did so and Gerry continued, "Quail are ground nesting and eat mainly insects, small seeds and grain. The local quail are spotted light gray and are known by the cute, semi-circular ringlet of flesh on the top of their head. The friendly animal you met on the trail was a skunk. With your usual unbelievable luck you were spared the unbearably nasty experience of being sprayed by a skunk. Their spray smells worse than anything else in the world! If you ever even smell it, you will become less eager to make friends." They were both getting tired and hungry so they agreed to continue later.

More Gold Mining School

The next morning at the mines Patches asked Gerry, "Why does the bank cave in when they wash out the dirt underneath it?" Gerry said, "Now is a good time to tell you more about placer mining. Besides the Giant there are other ways to wash away the soil and save the gold. One is with the miner's pan. It is made of steel, circular, flat-bottomed, with sloping sides. They half fill it with dirt and slosh it around to wash the dirt overboard and leave the gold in the bottom of the pan. Another way uses a thing called a rocker. It looks like a child's rocker, except that it has a hopper near the top where they put in dirt to be washed. It has riffles where the child's bed would have been which trap gold like a sluice box." Patches said, "Gerry you still haven't told me why the bank caves in." Gerry said, "Sorry Patches, the huge slab of dirt that breaks away weighs about 50 or 100 tons and simply pulls itself away from the remaining bank."

Back to the Bird Area

After the mining lessons Patches went home to one of Grandma's tasty snacks and a short nap. Next he was off to the bird area. As he entered, he met the skunk he had seen before. He bowed down showing that he wanted to play and the skunk did also. They wandered around in the bird area for a while and Patches asked the skunk if he would like to see the mines. The skunk was delighted with the idea. Patches introduced himself and said, "What is your name?" The skunk said, "My name is Stinky and I'm very glad to meet you, Patches." He added, "I guess I don't need to tell you why they call me that." "Nope, I guess not," Patches responded.

A Grand Tour of the Mines

None of the workers were around the mine right then so Patches showed and explained the equipment and its operation to his new friend. They started with the water reservoir where the water was collected for use in washing the earth away and exposing the gold, or trapping it for later collection. Next they saw how the water went through a ditch to a thing called a penstock. There, a huge tank gave some pressure to the water before it entered a large diameter pipeline. The pipe got gradually smaller, which added speed and pressure to the water. Then the water was sprayed under very high pressure by a machine called a Hydraulic Mining Giant. Lastly, the giant delivered a stream of water much like that from a huge fire hose. Then the mining was done much like we explained above.

When he told about riding the cave-in down, he said, "Don't be too quick to try it because my friend Gerry won't and he's really smart." Stinky said, "Don't worry, I sure won't." Patches asked, "Stinky, did you understand the things I tried to show and explain, or do you have any questions about the mines?" Stinky said, "I followed very closely and I think I have it down pat. Your tour was great, Thank you, Patches."

The Terrible Scare!

Patches thought he should take Stinky back to the bird area to be sure he knew the way. When they got there Patches saw someone with a shotgun! He told Stinky, "Go home fast!" When Stinky went in the trees Patches heard a shot, then silence! He feared for the skunks welfare. Then the hunter picked up a pheasant and left. It was a beautiful creature with many bright colors, an odd looking comb and a long graceful tail. It seemed like a terrible shame for someone to kill it. By then Patches felt like it was safe so he headed home.

When Patches told Gerry about Stinky, he was as mad as a hatter! Gerry said, "The first time I even smell a dad-ratted skunk there will be the Devil to pay!" Patches tried to tell him, "The skunk is nice if you are good to it." Gerry got even madder! When he was a pup, he had been sprayed by a darn skunk and he hadn't even known it was there. He told Patches to be sure it never returned and that was that. Patches figured he had better not push the matter any farther. The next morning Patches hunted up Stinky and said, "How would you like for me to show you around the area?" Stinky said, "Sure, that sounds great." About a half mile up the hill there was a small mahogany forest. Mahogany is a very tough hardwood, and some mahogany species are trees while some are bushes. It has gray-green, broad leaves and for some reason quail and pheasants like to nest there.

Farther up the hill a road winds around the side of a mountain in the pines. They followed the road past the trees and downhill through some sagebrush to some old, dilapidated buildings. Patches said, "This

97

used to be an old stamp mill that was used to pulverize rocks to find gold. The rock was mined out of steep tunnels and moved to the stamp mill in small ore cars, similar to a railroad." As they were leaving the stamp mill building, they met a porcupine. It started to turn and fill someone's nose with quills, but it saw Stinky and ran for dear life! It knew it didn't dare make the skunk mad. Patches knew that saved the day for both of them. One of the other buildings had been a mining cabin and to Stinky's delight he found some bird's eggs inside. He offered to share them but Patches respectfully declined.

When they left the house, they heard a terrible squawking noise. It seemed to be saying that they were in the wrong territory. Stinky didn't know what it was and he was so scared he could he could hardly breathe. Patches said, "Look up in that tree, it's a blue jay, it won't harm you. They are just annoying." The darn blue jay followed them everywhere they went and kept yapping its head off. Then Patches saw a huge hawk flying toward them. It went for the blue jay. They heard some dreadful noises for a few seconds but they couldn't see what happened. Then they didn't hear anything from the blue jay.

Where Have You Been?

That evening after supper Gerry was waiting for Patches. He said, "Everyone has been looking for you all day. We were worried sick thinking something bad had happened." Patches felt small enough to fall through a nail hole. He tried to let each and every soul involved know that he was sorry. Gerry told him to wait until morning, and then find the skunk and tell him how things were. The next morning Patches ate a few bites and was on his way to the bird area. It was his turn to worry, there was no sign of Stinky! He looked all through the bird area with no luck. Finally he saw some of his friend's fresh tracks. He desperately hoped things were OK. As he rounded a small knoll, he met two skunks. Stinky said, "Hello Patches, I'd like for you to meet my fiancee, Petunia." Patches bowed gracefully and said, "Hello Petunia, I'm really pleased to meet you. I can sense that each of you is ideally suited to the other. Before I have to go back to the mines, I want each of you to know, if I can ever do anything for you, please remember that I am your friend." Stinky said, "Thank you," and they touched paws. Petunia said, "Thank you very much, that was beautiful." Patches was so happy he nearly cried.

When Patches got back to the mines, Gerry was waiting for him again. When Patches mentioned the change of events Gerry was pleased as could be and all was well again. Then they went to the mining area just in time for Patches to ride down a cave-in. The others were tickled pink that he had returned safely.

Gerry's Bee Tree

A few days later it was Gerry's turn to worry everyone. There were lots of bees at the spring where the household water came from. He had noticed that after they drank they all flew away in the same direction. Gerry followed one as far as he could, then waited for another one. Finally they led him to an old pine tree with their nest and their honey supply. He was at a loss for what to do next and moped around like he had lost his best friend. Try as he might, Patches couldn't get a peep out of him.

At last Gerry went to the mine just as the men were taking a break. He began barking, then running a little ways up the trail, then barking again. Finally someone noticed and followed him. He led the way past the bird area and the mahogany forest, to the gooseberry patch. He could hear the bees but he knew the people couldn't hear them. He bravely went right up to the tree and scratched next to some bees. It worked! He knew the man was thinking about cutting the tree in the winter when the bees were hibernating. The man said, "C'mon Gerry, let's get the heck out of here!" When they got back to the house Gerry told Patches what had happened while the man did the same for the people.

That winter when there was about two feet of snow on the ground and it was way below zero outside, they decided to cut the tree. They took the things they would need to fell, buck and split the tree, as well as two buckets for the honey and plenty of warm clothing. (Lumberjacks use the term *buck* to mean cutting the tree into logs and to *fell* means to cut it down). The next morning before daylight they fell the tree. There was an almost never-ending crash, after which someone said, "Good golly, look at that!" The tree trunk was frozen so brittle that it snapped into four pieces when it fell. The next surprise was that two buckets weren't even a, "drop in the bucket," for the honey. The people decided to use a tarpaulin to slide the honeycombs to the house by pulling the load with the team of horses.

A few minutes later Patches started howling and scratching at his face. Some of the bees were arousing and he was the first thing they saw. The people were laughing themselves silly and Gerry was rolling in the snow with glee. Then Patches started burrowing in the snow and rubbing the bees off. He was also smart enough to make a, "beeline," for home. He was the first one back to the house for some of Grandma's treats. He thought, "Toughie for the rest of you laughing Jokers."

After the honeycombs were heated and the honey drained out there was over thirty gallons of pure, liquid honey!

Some Parting Thoughts

Patches and Gerry left a world of wonderful memories of things that brightened everyone's day, every day. If you listen closely up at the mines, you can hear Gerry laughing at Patches. It's a shame that many of their antics were later forgotten and are not a part of this story. Every reader has the chance to enjoy what there is and use his or her own imagination for the rest of the story of those wonderfully mischievous imps.

Many people have had their lives enriched by the adventures, joys and hardships in this story. The writer fondly hopes that the readers have enjoyed reading about mines and gold mining, and perhaps learned more than they had known about the subject.

VI

BUSTER THE PROUD POM

Buster was a light peach colored Pomeranian dog. He gave added meaning to words like brave, adventurous, fun loving and loyal. One might think of him as an odd looking, disagreeable, aggressive, yappy mutt. That idea is totally wrong. The truth is just as stated above. He had his own ideas and feelings. This story is told from his point of view. For example, the family pickup was <u>his</u> pickup. Often things he would have said if he could speak are in the story. He was annoyed because his part of the pickup seat was slippery and he kept sliding off. Someone fastened a large towel to the middle of the seat to give him traction. Boy he was proud. He thought, "I knew they could do it!"

Introduction

Buster had an exceptional ability to show his feelings or moods. When he was ready to fight or bite he would bare his teeth and give a blood curdling snarl, leaving no doubt with people or animals about how he felt. His actions and expressions plainly showed when he was mad, glad, sad or in just about any mood. He was the head of the household and often kept the family's three boys from killing each other. He also protected the mother from harm of any origin.

Part of the Family

The family often took Buster to the beach where he dearly loved to run the unobstructed five-mile stretch of smooth sand. While the people walked the full distance he circled around them and easily went several steps to each of theirs. He smelled everything along the way for miles. When it was hot, he liked to get his belly wet and shake water all over them. He wished he could smile and say, "How do you like that?" after giving them a deluge shower.

Buster dearly loved to play in the snow. Once he was in about four inches of snow and he jumped up and down until he was dog-tired and half frozen.

He was in the height of his glory. Another time he was gleefully snapping at snowflakes. Yep, he was still in his glory. Once the family took him fishing at the Lewis and Clark River. It runs west from Saddle Mountain State Park near Seaside, Oregon. He would try to catch fish in his mouth to make people proud of him. It didn't help people's fishing very much but he was so cute nobody could be angry with him.

Once he had so much fun he forgot his bearings and wandered downstream to where he saw a deer drinking water. He thought, "I know darned well I can catch that Devil! I'll really make them proud." He tried to catch it, but it could outrun him many times over. He must have got lost because he barked until someone came to his rescue. Then it was a tossup whether to hug him for letting them know, or wring his scrawny neck for being so dumb. Anyhow those were wonderful days for people and dogs.

Another time he suddenly came up missing in downtown Portland, Oregon. People searched frantically all day and night with no luck. Then someone saw movement in the middle of the street. Was it him? Then a closer look showed that it was! The poor little guy was dazed, lethargic, cold and soaked to the skin. Everyone was thrilled to learn that he was safe. Soon he was recovered and returned to his mischievous self. He had greatly benefitted by people's love and his fool luck. He wished he had a way to tell them he had been kidnaped and had managed to escape. He thought, "It just doesn't seem fair!" We humans quite often agree with his observation. It had been a terrifying ordeal for him. Luckily dogs can always find their way home **if** they have control of their faculties.

Perhaps some day we people will find a way to help them do so. Buster thought they would. He thought, "Look at all of the neat stuff they have done for us dogs already."

The Carpeted Stairway

When Buster was about twelve, he began suffering with arthritis. He liked to sleep on the bed where it was nice and warm, but he could hardly climb up. Someone built him a stairs, and even carpeted the steps so that he wouldn't slip or be afraid of slipping. When he gained enough confidence he walked up his stairs and he was proud as a kid with a new toy. The best part for him was knowing that they were *his* stairs and he went to all extremes letting people know how grateful he was. He thought, "It would be neat if they had put the name **BUSTER** on my new steps, but I'm grateful beyond expression as it is."

At the family home he often jumped up in the man's lap and tried to lick his nose, but he was always told, "Don't lick my nose!" He tried it when he got the new stairs, but he had the same luck. He thought, "Rats, there must be a way to do this!" The next day he got in the man's lap and laid quietly for a few moments then arose, stretched and yawned, then suddenly licked the man's nose! The man gave a hearty laugh and then hugged him. That was one of Buster's greatest moments.

Once he had lived where they had lots of farm animals that he helped watch over. Sometimes the chickens would escape from their coop and hide in the nearby bushes. He would herd them back home and be the hero. He would be in such high spirits from the praise he would get that he started unlatching the chicken house door with his paw or digging out under the fence to let them escape. The fun didn't last because the people got suspicious and caught him in the act. Then he got what hurt the worst. He was sternly scolded in a low, gentle voice. Gosh, he hated that! He was so terribly hurt by the disapproval of his people that the chickens no longer got loose. He thought, "Rats, I knew they would catch me!"

There were some goats on the place that were tied to a tree so that they couldn't run away and get into trouble. They would walk one way to the end of their rope, then cry for someone to walk them the other way to unwind the rope. When they did it repeatedly, Buster thought, "I can't believe they're that stupid!" Yet he knew they were experts at opening gates and doors, without his help. He wondered, "Which are the dumbest, goats or chickens?" It seems doubtful that we or he will ever know.

Be Sure to Lock Up

There were two grain boxes in one of the sheds, one for chicken feed and the other for goat feed. The boys did the feeding and sometimes they would forget to weigh down the box lids. There were always some chipmunks around, patiently waiting for that to happen. Chipmunks are magicians at opening containers by shaking jar lids or raising the covers, etc. Then they were smart enough to climb inside and eat the feed, but they weren't smart enough to climb back out. They would chatter loudly until Buster heard them and barked for someone to come to their rescue. Then someone would dip them out with the feed can. Buster spent endless hours watching their antics and showing a facial expression of total disbelief.

The people had a little kitten named Bandit. It had cute markings much like a raccoon. It was very curious and mischievous, and was always in trouble. Buster and Bandit were very close friends and they had endless hours of fun teasing the other animals. There was a neatly stacked pile of wood near the house. Sometimes the teasing worked both ways because the chipmunks would hide in the woodpile and tease Bandit while he was too little to deal with them, until he was big enough to chase them off.

Then Bandit told Buster, "Look Buzzy, now *I'm* the king of the hill. Buster was happy to see Bandit so proud at last. After that the chipmunks had their hands full when they tried to tease Bandit. He was both smart and tough. He could quickly make them scurry for the woodpile. Sadly, something bad must have happened to Bandit. He stopped coming around and they never knew why.

One day the youngest boy in the family shot Buster with a rubber band gun. His mom scolded him and he watched for the chance to do it again. When he did, Buster bit him and made his lip bleed. Buster felt awful, but he still thought, "I know where I would like to put that stupid rubber band gun!" Anyhow, boy lived...dog lived...no more problem.

Buster's people moved to a place that he dearly loved, way out in the country, where they wound up with two kittens. One was a boy who acted tough and they called him Toughy. The other was a girl with extra long whiskers who they called Whiskers. Buster was both a friend and a parent to both of them. He showed them around the place and taught them how to recognize and avoid persons or animals that might harm them. He told them, "Stay away from the road so you won't get hit by the cars and trucks." He spent endless hours licking them. People thought it was cute but they didn't know how horrible cats tasted and smelled to a dog. Still he had loads of fun with them and they were the same as his babies.

One day Toughie came up missing and was nowhere to be found. Like Bandit, no one knew why but he simply never came back. After that Buster and Whiskers were nearly inseparable. By then Buster's vision was getting quite weak and Whiskers started acting as his, "Seeing-Eye-Cat," as though he was her favorite child. Sometimes he would stray toward the road and she would move up beside him and crowd him the other way, toward safety. If he didn't eat and drink like he should, she would push him toward his dish. She had an uncanny sense of what was needed for his welfare. It was interesting that he would obey a cat and seemed to be grateful. The people were grateful also.

Buster had a compelling appetite for spaghetti and he would have given his soul for the stuff, especially if someone would lower a long piece so it would slide down his throat. As silly as it sounds, people have had endless hours of pleasure watching that performance. He enjoyed many more good days with Whisker's help and care than he would have without her, thanks to her loving tenderness and amazing wisdom. Buster and his cat friends brightened people's lives in so many ways. They all deserve a special place in their heavenly happy hunting grounds.

VII

A DOG NAMED ZY

Whoever heard of a dog named Zy? How do you pronounce it? Where does he live? What does he like to do? Who are his friends? How is he special? Kids of all ages will have the chance for a lot of education and amusement in this unusual tale which was adapted from real life in Southeast Alaska. Fasten your easy chair belts and enjoy.

Introduction

Two people named Lee and Anne lived in Southeast Alaska in the town of Klawok. It is located on Prince of Wales Island, about 70 miles west of Ketchikan. Ketchikan is located on Revillagigedo Island, 235 miles south of Juneau, 90 miles north of Prince Rupert, BC, and 600 miles north of Seattle, WA.

The story opens as Lee and Anne are looking for a dog for a pet and for protection. Someone wanted to sell a small male puppy so they went to look at him. It was love at first sight for them and the dog. He was part Alaskan Husky and part German Shepard. He had a thin, shiny black coat and held

113

his ears upright, plus his tail curved upward. He was a beautiful dog and seemed to always have a beaming smile. Lee noticed that the dog had giant feet. He said, "He won't need snow shoes." His broad shoulders and deep chest gave him good wind and great strength. The bright gleam in his eyes made him appear friendly, yet alert. The people selling the dog said he could be trained for whatever they wanted him to do.

Lee asked what they called him and was told, "Zy." He said, "Do you mean like a deep sigh?" He was told, "Yep." Lee asked, "Why in the world would you call him that?" The lady said, "We thought he was one of a kind." The man said, "Lee, I'm afraid you're stuck with it. If you call him by name, he responds right away. If you don't use his name, he'll pretend not to hear you. He is easy to teach, just, "Show-and-Tell" him a time or two and he will learn. He can even count, Zy get me two sticks of wood." With two quick trips Zy brought the two sticks and laid them at the man's feet. The man patted him on the head. The woman said, "Zy, go lay down. He lies on his old coat on the porch."

Lee said, "You folks will miss him around here." Then he said, "Can I have that old coat?" The man said, "Sure Lee, he seems to love that old thing." Lee tossed the coat on the back of the pickup bed and started to call Zy. Anne said, "Wait Lee, let's make him comfortable." She smoothed the coat out and placed it next to the cab for a windbreak, then said, "OK now teach him to jump in." Lee lowered the tailgate and patted it as a signal, whereupon Zy jumped up with no words spoken. That was the beginning of the deepest bond between a human and a beast. Zy thought, "This is the finest thing that has ever happened to me."

Early the next morning Lee went to work with Zy in his place in the pickup bed. When he got to work, he got out and said, "Zy stay," pointing to the coat, then went to work with the dog guarding his master's rig. Thus began each work day for Lee and Zy.

Hello, Phoenix Log Shop

Lee worked as a heavy equipment mechanic for Phoenix Logging Company at Klawok, Alaska, in the Tsongas National Forest. The parent company was Phoenix Logging Company at Phoenix, Oregon, near Medford. The town of Klawok is about half way up the west coast of the island. The town of Klawok has about 600 people and, like the rest of the island, relies on timber and fishing as the main source of income. In bygone days the island had produced untold fortunes in gold and silver, but like most of the wild west, it was long-since mined out.

The island is about 130 miles long north to south and is about 30 miles wide. The climate is similar to Seattle, except that during most winters it has at least a foot of snow and is a little bit colder.

Generally Zy stayed in the pickup while Lee worked. Nobody even looked toward Lee's pickup or the thousands of dollars worth of tools stored inside. Zy was familiar with the people who worked at the company's heavy equipment repair shop and he wagged his tail when they passed by. Zy had a different bark when he wanted down from his perch and Lee would say, "Zy, get down." Then he would run and play anywhere within sight of the pickup. If Lee started toward the rig, Zy would beat him to it and be in his place for a ride.

During the winter Zy was allowed indoors in Lee and Anne's trailer, early in the morning and in the evening. He stayed on his own rug while the others ate but the rest of the time indoors was his playtime. He liked to roughhouse with his people and he dearly loved to romp in the snow. He could easily run circles around anyone who would go along. The rest of his body size soon caught up with his feet and he started sinking in the snow. Lee said, "It looks like I might have to see about those snowshoes." Lee and Anne made sure he had enough fun playing to make up for the time guarding the pickup in whatever sort of weather the heavens above offered. When Anne wanted to use the pickup, she took Lee to work, then she and Zy were on their way. She would let him ride in the cab while the pickup was moving but he went back to his old coat while it was parked. When she put goods from the store in the pickup, Zy wanted to see every item. Apparently he wanted to make sure it was OK, then he didn't worry.

Zy strongly disliked the horrible tasting water found in most of Alaska. It tastes brackish, which means salty or nauseating. He wasn't alone, people hated it too. He was most grateful that Lee and Anne always gave him plenty of good tasting water. The water came from a huge rainwater collection tank. Once a week it was Anne's chore to get their water supply from the tank. The tank was nearly as large as a railroad gondola and had been cleaned and lined inside to make it safe and suitable for storing potable household water. Anne and Zy would take all of their water containers to the water tank on the pickup and fill them with a hose provided for the purpose. The tank was supported on a platform high enough for the water to run out. You can bet that Anne never complained about the chore. She said she usually stayed dry and wasn't affected much by the cold, except in the winter when the weather was cold and windy. Then she would nearly always spill water all over herself. She said the great-tasting water was worth any amount of suffering.

Zy Loved to Fly

Once Lee took Zy along on a trip to Sitka. You can't go there by land because they don't have highways on the ocean, so travel is by ferryboat or air, so they flew. On takeoff Zy was scared at first but Lee looked relaxed when the power was reduced from takeoff to climb, then to cruise, which made the ride much smoother and quieter. Zy thought, "This is the ONLY way to fly!" First they flew from Thorne Bay, on the east side of the island, to Ketchikan in a De Haviland Otter. It was a float plane, (with pontoons), and was propellor driven. It was greatly overpowered for safety in critical situations. Lee and Zy experienced one of those. They were making a stop at a small Indian fishing village on an island where they were caught by some fierce wind gusts. They surely would have piled up on some rocks, save for a very savvy bush pilot. He used full throttle and full rich mixture quickly enough to recover and sustain flight. Lee was as white as a sheet and Zy put his paws over his eyes. Zy thought, "I'm not going until my time comes, but it may be near at hand." For a moment the Otter had nearly stalled in midair, but then it climbed nearly straight up and gained speed, with no apparent strain except for a loud exhaust roar and more vibration than usual. Their landing at Ketchikan was as smooth as anyone could hope for and Zy was all smiles. He must have been the proudest dog in Alaska. Their touchdown was like landing on a mattress and taxiing was like a canoe ride. It was one of those days when it was beautiful, both during the flight and on the water.

They were in Ketchikan barely long enough to change aircraft, but Zy nearly managed to get into a fight with a smart-mouth dog that made fun of the name Zy. Lee pulled them apart and took Zy over to the Concourse, then Lee got in a row for refusing to put Zy in a pet carrier and shipping him as cargo, in an extremely cold cargo bay. The people in charge soon decided it would be wiser to accommodate the man's wishes and let the dog ride in the cabin. Zy thought that was a swell idea. He wagged his tail and snuggled up tightly against Lee.

Zy loved the smoother ride and his high perch in the larger aircraft where he could see far and wide. He wasn't prepared for the forward thrust of an MD-80's engines on takeoff. Lee said the dog managed to avoid making even a whimper during liftoff and he readily settled down when the power was reduced to the climb and cruise settings. He soon realized that he wasn't going to die so he looked out at the fast sinking ground and found himself en route to doggie heaven. He smiled like he was riding in the pickup cab on a hot day with his head out of the window and eating an ice cream cone.

Sitka is on Barinof Island, 185 air miles north of Ketchikan. Its climate is similar to Prince of Wales Island. Zy wanted to stay longer at Sitka because everything was so beautiful, but Lee was there after repair parts and they had to go right back. At least Zy did get to see the pride of Sitka, which was their Mac Donalds Drive-in, also the city's one traffic light. Zy thought, "Fiddlesticks, this doesn't seem fair!" He had to settle for the notion that both flights were the experience of a lifetime for him.

The Deserted Gold Mine

Another time Lee took Zy to a former mine called the Salt Chuck Mine on the west coast of Prince of Wales Island. Many years earlier it had been an underground gold mine. Lee showed him the ore cars and their tracks which had carried thousands of tons of gold ore out of the mine. Also he showed Zy a thing called a, "Jackleg," or a pneumatic drill for drilling upwards in rock. Next they went through what seemed like miles of tunnels. Zy thought, "Wow, this place sure seems spooky to me!" There was water dripping from the overhead everywhere.

Zy was uneasy with the notion that the whole place might cave in at any moment, and he sure was glad when they were starting to leave. He thought, "I've learned a little more than I think I needed to Know."

Otter Fish?

Lee and Zy both had a precious memory of a trip to Thorne River on the east side of the island. Lee was fishing, using plastic worms for bait and he kept feeling light tugs on the line, but he wasn't catching any fish. Then he noticed some otters watching him from the riverbank. He realized they were yanking on the line and enjoying his frustration. Zy was frustrated also because Lee was having poor luck. Finally Lee managed to catch some four inch minnows. He bought some fish on the way home. He wasn't afraid of his wife Anne, he was simply hungry for fish.

Equipment Breakdowns

Most of Lee's work entailed repairing equipment on the job, where it had broken down. Many lesser men avoided working out in the snow, mud, rain, etc., to enable the company work to continue. Every employee's income depended upon delivering logs to fill a contract. When production stops, you have trouble paying your bills and buying food. Lee had to make the repairs at the site without moving the machinery to the shop, unless it was totally impossible. That was always a nearly insurmountable task.

Observations in Passing

Zy had many, "at-a-distance," friends, but they stayed well clear of Lee and Anne's things. Zy gave his undying loyalty with every breath. He was a special creature in so many ways, especially in caring for his people. Lee, Anne and Zy loved each other beyond anyone's wildest imagination. Their lives were always good because of the way they treated and regarded each other. They spent several years in southeast Alaska and gathered a treasure of memories, plus some beautiful fish and even some gold.

This writer strongly feels that everyone should at least visit Alaska and Hawaii during their lifetime. With that said, a word of caution seems in order before going to Alaska. Some facilities along the highways of the North-land may be a bit on the rustic side. There are a myriad of perils that can entrap or inconvenience the unwary, and one of the best ways to avoid lots of trouble is to obtain information about traveling and living in the area.

One great source of such knowledge is a book called *THE MILEPOST*. It is known as the bible of North Country travel. For information about this publication, contact the Alaska Northwest Publishing Company, 130 2nd Ave., South, Edmonds, Washington, 98020. Phone 1 (800) 533-7381.

Zy finally found a lady friend and settled down to doing his part to raise a litter of puppies who looked and acted just like him. There's no telling what might happen if you went to Prince of Wales Island and called loudly to Zy!

VIII

DIAMOND EYED SPOT

Spot was a ranch dog, much like you'd expect to find with a country family who raised livestock. He was taller than a Spaniel, but shorter than a German Shepard. He was solid white from head to toe, except for a black patch around his left eye that was diamond shaped. The ranch was called the Diamond Eye Ranch, as inspired by Spot when he was a small pup. All of the people for miles around knew Spot and the Diamond Eye Ranch. Young and old alike had a great love for that adorable creature.

The Family

People for miles around knew the family and their story in the area. The father, Tom Wheeler had been born and raised at the same ranch house as his father, Everett Wheeler. His grandfather, John Wheeler, had homesteaded the place in the nineteenth century. Tom still lived in the same place with his wife and children. Being a more modern family, the children were born in town.

The mother, Nancy Wheeler, was born and raised on a ranch about ten miles from Tom's place. They had been childhood sweethearts and had married when they graduated from high school. They had two children, a daughter Evelyn who was ten at the time of this story. Also their son Charles, was eight at the time. Finally, our hero, Diamond Eyed Spot was born out in the barn about three years previously.

Besides the family, other principal persons who worked to solve the mystery and conclude the business at hand included the following; Tom's brother, Bob Wheeler on the state police force, led their investigation. Sheriff Bill Kelsay and his team helped with other details as much as possible. Sheriff's Lieutenant Williams supervised the sheriff's department's efforts in the case. Also the state police had a Captain Monty Hartford who was Superintendent of Interrogation at the state capital.

Peace and Quiet

The story begins with Spot sunning himself on the front porch while the family was in church. He loved the peace and quiet while they were gone. The only disturbance was a magpie squawking at some little birds that were scratching for food in the barnyard. All else was still except for the water trickling in the creek behind the house. Spot was expecting the family home from church before long.

He heard a vehicle coming up the road, but something seemed wrong. He felt uneasy and thought, "Who are these people and why are they coming here?" Soon a dilapidated old pickup came into view, followed by a cloud of dust. It had a beat up looking canopy with no windows. It turned off of the county road and onto the driveway, which worried Spot more than ever. His instincts were telling him to run for cover, but his duty was to look after things while his people were away.

The pickup stopped and two rough looking men climbed out and walked straight toward the house. One called, "Here Spot!" Poor Spot ran for dear life for the barnyard where there were several ways to escape. He thought, "How in the Devil do they know my name? Why did they call me? Above all, How can I avoid capture?" He led them through a maze of cross-fences to the lower ground in the barnyard with its awful sticky stuff that collects on your shoes. He slid under the fence at full speed, and greatly added to his lead over the two men. Soon he was in the foliage by the creek, safely out of their view. He knew where he could hide in an old badger hole by the creek, but when he started to crawl inside he heard a bloodcurdling growl. Suddenly he thought, "Holy cow! The darned badger is at home!" Then he backed out, right into the hands of one of the two men! Then he thought,

"Rats, of all of the rotten luck! This mess is going from bad to worse!" At that point, what was the worst problem, the badger or the two men? Then he was poked into a gunnysack and given a free ride to the pickup. Spot was at a total loss to understand any of the events or to even guess what was next. The men quickly put him in the canopy and made their getaway. He could hear their voices but he couldn't tell what they were saying. What could he do to protect himself? How could he leave some sign for the people who would want to help him?

It seemed like the most mysterious thing was the two men. He knew they had nothing in mind that would be good for him. They surely must be outlaws or bandits of some sort. Actually, **bandits** seemed to fit extra well.

The old pickup streaked out of the driveway, then headed toward town on the county road. After what seemed like forever they turned up the hill on a bumpy, rutted dirt road. The gunnysack slid all over the pickup bed with Spot and he was slammed into the sides, and the junk in the back of the bed.

Where is Spot?

When the family got home from church, they saw tracks in the driveway showing they had been visited while they were gone. They called Spot but got silence. He had been on the front porch when they left. Why wasn't he still there? Was there a connection between their missing pet and the mysterious visitor? Could someone have taken Spot? If so, who and why? More importantly, what could be done to learn the facts and come to his aid if there was a need?

The father, Tom Wheeler, said, "All bases must be covered as soon as possible. I'll get Sheriff Bill Kelsay, to start a search and get my brother Bob, on the State Police to start the detective work. Everyone must stay indoors to avoid disturbing any sign or evidence." He knew the hardest thing was to do nothing, but Spot's very life might depend on exactly that. He said, "We can do a few things in the meanwhile. You kids can write a description and gather some pictures of Spot for any searchers. Anything you can do may help. Mother you may need to provide food and shelter for wall-to-wall people for a few days. Meanwhile I'll be able to keep plenty busy planning our next moves."

Hiram Smith's Laborer's Cabin

When the pickup reached the top of the hill the road flattened out and the ground was nice and level, giving Spot a smooth ride...for the last few yards. One of the men said, "I'll go inside and scrape up some vittles if you'll put Spot in the doghouse and give him some water and dog food." Spot didn't have the answer to one darn question but he knew he must keep in shape and watch for a chance to escape. He thought, "After that wild ride in the gunnysack I'm sure lucky to be safe and sound, and that dogs can always find their way home." After the bandits finished their supper and rinsed the dishes they wasted no time going to bed because they knew the next day would be busy. Soon the snoring was clearly audible over the whistling wind, the rattling doors and the other nameless nighttime sounds. Someone had left a sleeping bag in the doghouse where Spot slept as-snug-as-a-bug-in-a-rug all night.

The next morning Spot peeked out of a crack in the wall and was astonished that it was bright daylight, and the bandits were already up and about. It had rained all night and the cabin roof had leaked on his hosts. They were grumbling about, "That lucky mutt in the doghouse." One of them came out and said, "Here Spot." Then put a collar and a tether on him and propped the door open. Then he brought out fresh food and water. On the spur of the moment Spot couldn't think of anything he hated worse than a collar and a leash. He heard them saying, "We should be hearing something from our partners pretty soon, then we'll know how to handle this."

The other said, "Yeah I suppose. I doubt if there's enough food here for another day." The first one responded, "We got a lucky break with the weather, there was probably enough rain to wash our tracks out on the hill. Maybe we should use the horses and meet with the others." Spot thought, "Rats, all of this talk tells me exactly nothing." He wondered, "What will the next dandy surprise be?"

Getting Organized

Sheriff Kelsay had arrived at the Tom Wheeler farmhouse and started to marshal people's activities. He was talking to the father about what was going on and what should happen next. He said, "Tom, you seem to have things pretty well organized, why don't you run the whole show from here?" The father, Tom Wheeler said, "Sure, I'll be pleased to, Sheriff." The sheriff added, "I'm glad your brother is involved. He has worked untold miracles in the past and you can bet he'll get to the bottom of this puzzle before long. Now, how about letting your two wonderful children coordinate everyone's communications?" Tom responded, "That's a dandy idea Bill, they're chomping at the bit to help!" The sheriff set up a two-way radio and gave the kids the call signs they would need. He turned on the radio just as the State Police were calling in. The sheriff answered and turned the call over to the kids. They dealt with the call like true professionals. The police said two suspects had been chasing the dog and had caught him behind the barn. They had carried him to the front and to their vehicle. They left some good footprints and tire tracks, of which the police made plaster casts. There were no other clues yet. The sheriff said he would have a helicopter cover a fifty square mile area for anything suspicious looking.

One of the kids was detailed to phone all of the neighbors in a twenty-mile radius for anyone who might have seen Spot. Charles got the job, and he asked the fire department for a map of the area mentioned. Then he simply circled the area on the map and called everyone who lived within the circle. Charles spoke to two neighbors who had seen the dilapidated pickup with two unknown men inside and reported it to his father.

Tom asked the State Police to run a computer check for persons in the county with· records for crimes that might be involved in this case, and to have Spot's description and picture broadcast statewide on television. Meanwhile the sheriff's deputies were canvassing nearby homes for anyone who had noticed unusual events that could be linked to Spot or the family. Then Tom radioed the sheriff and his brother and said, "I'd like for us to meet this evening at my house for supper and to review progress and summarize what is known."

Present for the evening meal were four state policemen, six deputy sheriffs, six neighbors and four family members. After the meal the father asked for reports from the various leaders. His brother Bob was first, He said, "Two men caught and removed Spot from the ranch. We have clear plaster casts and footprints from the driveway, around the buildings and in the yard. Computer runs will be available within the hour to identify persons with records for embezzlement, extortion, kidnaping and other crimes that could be involved in this case. The next speaker was Sheriff's Lieutenant Williams. During interviews at nearby homes two people had reported a strange vehicle in the area and had given similar descriptions of the dilapidated pickup, including mention of two unfamiliar men inside. That information coincided with Charles' report from the same two people. He said he had just given the descriptions to the chopper pilot.

The Deserted Smith Place

When the two bandits met with the others at the main house, they were told that the sheriff and the state police were involved and that the plan would have to be altered, but that no harm was done. They were to ride their two horses back for the dog and leave everything else alone, without any fingerprints. The pickup was stolen from Mexico City and could not be traced. They must use the same route to and from the cabin and leave the paved road at the creek, then wade the horses out to avoid leaving tracks. They were to return to the main house afterward and wait for further orders. The bandits said they needed food for themselves and the dog but they were told to make no side trips. Supplies would be in place when they arrived, plus they were told to stay indoors in the daytime because such simple lapses had tripped up others in the past. It would be dark when they got back to the cabin and they dared not to turn on any lights, but they must be thorough in removing fingerprints.

The Demands!

The next day the mailman put one letter in the mailbox for the Diamond Eye Ranch. When Tom opened it, his mouth fell open. He looked like he had seen a ghost! It read, "We have your dog and when you fully obey our instructions he will be returned unharmed. You must do the following, exactly:

- Stop all law enforcement and search efforts.

- Make no effort to get help or to contact anyone.
- Put $50,000 in small, unmarked bills in the mailbox at the vacant Smith place and lock the box, using the open padlock inside.
- Make the delivery tomorrow in the daytime.
- You can guess the penalty for failure.

People were arriving at the ranch for another planning and progress meeting. The father called his brother Bob and the sheriff aside before the meal and advised them of the ransom note. After they finished eating, he said he was canceling the meeting. He said, "I've learned that Spot will be returned unharmed. If that proves true, there's no sense in further disrupting people's lives. My family and I are most grateful for all of your efforts and we are extremely relieved that everything is working out so well." The people were speechless and in shock at what the father had said. It seemed mighty odd that he was quitting with no answers or explanations to the whole mystery. They all said they would be pleased to do more. Soon they said their farewells and left.

When Tom finished accepting offers of help and trying to convince the others that things were well in hand, it was late and he went to bed.

When the two bandits returned to the cabin, it was pitch dark and Spot was whining for food and water. It was cloudy with no moon so they knew it would be hopeless to try to remove their fingerprints before morning. They fed and watered Spot and the horses and locked them out of sight, then enjoyed a nice cold snack and went to bed.

Spot's Big Chance!

Spot awoke at about 4:00 A.M. when it was just getting daylight. He could hear snoring from the cabin so he thought it would be a good time to escape. He couldn't loosen any of the wallboards or raise the roof, then he thought, "Wow, I'm dumb!" The soil under the doghouse was sandy and it took him less than a minute to dig out, and then he was gone in a flash! He soon was well on his way home but he met a chain of obstacles and didn't get to the ranch house driveway until after dark. He thought, "This might be just as well, maybe it is better if I am unseen." When he climbed upon the porch he raised a terrible fuss until he heard the kids running to open the door. They yelled, "Look everyone, Spot's home!" That was enough said, the place was in complete pandemonium while they all exchanged greetings and gratitude. Spot still had no answers but he knew everything was well from his point of view.

At the ranch four persons had stayed after the father said the meeting was canceled. Besides Sheriff Kelsay and Bob Wheeler, he had quietly asked the two neighbors who had seen the dilapidated pickup to join in a new meeting. The father said, "I feel we had a spy in our midst at the last meeting and our radio calls may be monitored with a scanner. Lets keep radio use to a minimum, use the telephone instead and discuss nothing about the investigation with anyone except those present now or law enforcement personnel. The telephone is very well suited to most of our needs. Folks that's all I have this time. Unless anyone has more business now, thanks to all and we can all use some sleep."

What do you Mean he's gone?

At the cabin the bandits awoke at about 8:00 A.M. and the sun was well up in the sky. They had coffee and toast while they discussed what to do next. They knew the horses and dog were OK so they began removing the fingerprints from everything in the cabin. It was 9:00 A.M. when they went outside to tend the animals. The one who was to care for the dog went to the barn and yelled, "He's gone!" The other one said, "What do you mean he's gone?" The reply was, "He dug out." Just then they heard a helicopter overhead. They were out of view in the shed and saw the chopper hover over the pickup for a few moments and then leave. They quickly made sure there were no more fingerprints, and then left on the horses. They had to disregard the order to hide in the daytime. They wore two cowboy hats that they had found in the shed and left the way they had came.

Just after takeoff the chopper radioed in about the dilapidated pickup, giving its description and location. Three deputies responded and met at the bottom of the hill to check for tracks. They found the horse tracks but couldn't tell which way they had gone on the paved road. While two of them went up the hill, the other one checked both directions on the paved road for any sign of the bandits. Close to one ranch he noticed two cowboys riding from the creek toward some ranch buildings. They were unfamiliar so he acted unconcerned until he was out of sight, then radioed in their descriptions. He also said where he saw them and where they went.

No Heroes Yet

When the two bandits rode into their meeting place, the others were waiting for them. One said, "I see you forgot to hide in the daytime and to bring the dog." They simply told what had happened.

When they mentioned the chopper, they got stone cold looks. Just then someone called out from the house and said, "The chopper pilot just called in and reported the pickup. Also a patrol car called in and reported seeing two cowboys, with their descriptions and where they went, which was here."

The state police phoned the father and told him of the two radio calls about the dilapidated pickup and the two cowboys. Bob Wheeler was there when the call came in. He said, "We can't trade jobs because I'm too dumb to run a ranch, but you'd make a heck of a good cop. I'd like to use your phone to get the crime lab started up at the cabin." The response was, "Go ahead, and I don't want your job."

The next morning Tom went to the bank and arranged for a $50,000 loan. He wanted to throw the culprits off of the track if they were watching his movements. He attended to some ongoing business in town, and then went back to the bank with a brief case to pick up the money. Next he went to his Safe Deposit Box and traded the money for some important papers and went home. There he traded his personal papers for some old newspapers, which he put in the Smith place mailbox, and locked it as instructed. Tom thought to himself, "I wish I could be hidden and watching whoever gathers their spoils."

The New Plan

When he returned home his brother called. The father interrupted and told him about the mailbox ploy. Then he said, "I wonder if you could stop by for a visit, just in case those folks don't appreciate their surprise. In fact I'm going to call our key law enforcement people for a special meeting. I'll be prepared by the time everyone is here." When they had all arrived, the father's brother Bob said, "There is progress at the cabin. The dilapidated pickup was stolen in Mexico City and can't be traced. There were clear fingerprints on the canopy latch handle and on a tin can in the cabin. The prints were of a prison parolee with a record for embezzlement, larceny and extortion. They belonged to the veterinarian. One of the detectives learned that the vet was nearly bankrupt and that the former owner of the Smith place was his uncle, Hiram Smith. The vet's name was not Tom Jones, but Thomas Alva Edison DeHart. We now know one of the culprits and why the crime was committed. The computer printout listed four possible suspects in the county, besides Tom DeHart. They all live within 20 miles of the Diamond Eye Ranch. One was Harvey Reed, the foreman of the Moss place. We doubt that he is involved due to his reputation and his work record. Besides he is using his correct name. Next are Ralph and Larry Barnett, who have been sharecropping the Collins place for over three years. They are suspects in some rustling in the area but we don't have a shred of proof. Lastly Cub Collins, who contracted to the sharecroppers. We just learned that the Barnett brothers, Cub Collins and Tom DeHart served time together in Joliet, Illinois. I must caution you that they are innocent until proven guilty in court, therefore publicly naming them would jeopardize any case we may have against them."

Now for Plan B

Tom said, "We need to decide what to do next. Now that Spot is home we can redirect some of our efforts and perhaps release some of our manpower. We are using all available resources, at a significant risk to the rest of the people in the area. I think we can cut down most of the sheriff's people. The State Police are much better manned and have plenty of funds. They also have statewide jurisdiction and more expertise in crime detection and criminal apprehension. I don't mean to belittle the Sheriff's Department. They are very limited on funds and they do a tremendous job for the resources they have. I'd like comments from my brother and the sheriff, then we can plan our future efforts." The sheriff spoke first, "I totally agree with what you said. I hope to return to my normal duties with all of my people. I want you to know that we will quickly and gladly respond to any need. I give my heartfelt thanks for the pleasant cooperation we have enjoyed up to this point. Thanks again to one and all." The State Policeman said, "I fully agree with both of you and I'm most grateful for all of your efforts, including my brother's insightful leadership. Now I guess it's time for a new plan."

Plan C

The way things stood the family was hindered by having fewer people available, while the gang was hampered by the loss of their spy and the ability to eavesdrop with the scanner. They didn't know that Spot was already home so they still hoped for a donation in the mailbox. The veterinarian had been watching for the dog from his place but he had nothing to report. He had been on the phone when Spot returned.

The father said, "You folks shouldn't make a mass exodus from here, that would draw attention to our reduced operations. Now Mother, could you scrape up some of your wonderful Cinnamon Rolls and coffee?" He continued, "I think we can save time by scaring or conning someone among the suspects. If we can pick the weakest link in the chain, maybe he'll snitch on the others. I say exclude Harvey Reed, he made a mistake and paid the penalty. He has dealt fair and square with folks in the area. I feel any or all of the others may be involved." His brother said, "Again I agree, the vet needed money and is most likely the leader. The Barnett brothers will stick together and won't snitch on each other. That leaves us with Cub Collins, and I think he will prove to be the weak link in the chain. By a handy coincidence, I want to pick him up for questioning about cattle rustling, with the others being unaware. We have footprints and tire tracks placing Cub, his pickup and livestock trailer at the scene of the latest rustling. I want to confer with the State Attorney General about dropping the charges for either rustling or extortion, if Cub is willing to make a deal and give information on the others." The father said, "There you go again Bob, stealing my ideas. Now let's see you make it work."

The next morning the State Police arrested Cub Collins at his home and took him to the State Capital for questioning. He was a seasoned criminal who had been extensively trained in prison on dealing with law enforcement personnel. The State Police had a Captain Monty Hartford in charge of interrogation who was also very well trained. At first Cub Collins wouldn't give the correct time of day, but within four hours he sank the boat for the whole mob. Later the Barnett brothers, Tom DeHart and Cub Collins were sent to prison for rustling and extortion. The veterinarian Tom DeHart was the leader. Ironically, all but the vet were doing well in their honest endeavors. Crime doesn't pay!

Back on the Diamond Eye Ranch, Spot had overheard enough to know who had held him a prisoner, and why. Now he had reverted to his normal role of greeting visitors, and calming and comforting the family. He was cautious about greeting visitors, and was careful to save time for sunning himself on the front porch. He dearly loves the peace and quiet while the family is in church, and the water trickling in the creek behind the house. If he could speak, he very likely would say, "Life sure is great!"

IX

MEET WOOFER

Woofer is a Black Labrador and German Shepard dog. He is also the most important part of the family. Now, let's imagine that he can think much the same as we humans, also we know that animals communicate with each other.

We will tune in on him and he will tell us how we can tell him from any ordinary mutt. Woofer is telling his neighbor dog, "It seems that people like my gray and black short hair and my eternally friendly smile. I am very proud of the things that I own, like the family pickup, my corner of the porch, a no-spill dish, four throw rugs and one Frisbee. I love to take the people's kids swimming, fishing, hiking, berry picking and to the playground for a game of Frisbee. I have a world of fun with the slide, the sand box and the Merry-Go-Around. I stop kid fights, arguments, street games and rough play indoors. I have a special bark to warn of danger and my ordinary bark is a low-toned mild roar. As soon as you hear it you'll know its Woofer!"

Otherwise, he's a wonderful creature.

The name *Woofer* is pronounced like book or look. He is such a pleasant animal to be around that people lavish affection on him wherever he goes. He stays in such a good mood because his family is so loving toward him. Woofer loves them equally in return. They spare no effort or expense to accommodate his needs or to come to his rescue in any emergency. When there is something wrong he is likely to be near at hand, like a bratty kid.

Woofer's story is presented from his point of view. Woofer's grammar "ain't" so good, but if you try you can understand his thoughts or messages. By the way, be sure to have fun while you are at it.

WOOFER'S ADVENTURES

Trapped in a Tree

When Woofer was a young pup the kids taught him to climb a ladder and before long he managed to climb a tree in the back yard. He thought "This is the dumbest idea in the whole world! If God wanted me to go up a tree I'd have wings! Oh well, I might as well go along with this nonsense". He simply used the tree limbs in the same manner as the ladder steps. He had to admit that he truly loved being able

145

to see all of the action in all directions. He thought "Wow, this is neat".

One day the kids took him out to the back woods near their home where they liked to play. He thought "These kids won't know or care if I do my own thing while they probably get into more trouble as usual. I'm going to see what they think is so great about this place". Woofer was sniffing around near a blackberry patch when he frightened a pheasant, causing it to take flight. Woofer had heard the sudden and terrifying sound of their wings when they took off so he wasn't scared this time. He thought, "I wondered what those things looked like, they're beautiful". It landed near the top of a pine tree and he started climbing after it. He had an awful time jumping up to the lowest limbs but he finally managed and soon was nearly within reach of the bird. It flew on to the next tree and Woofer was scared to climb back down. He wished he could fly but he simply could not. He also thought "I wish I could get my hands on that 'beautiful' creature! It makes me mad to think I'll have to try to get the kids to help me. I'm supposed to be smarter than they are". He began making a pitiful howl that attracted the kids. When they started to climb up after him he made a worse fuss than ever. One of them asked the neighbors to call the Fire Department for help. Soon they came out with a big red ladder truck, but they couldn't get the truck close enough for the ladder to reach the tree. After several tries they called the police who suggested calling the National Guard for a helicopter to do the job.

Meanwhile poor Woofer had been hanging on so long he was about to fall out of the tree. He could imagine how his life would be if all the other dogs heard about this mess. Then he heard the swish-swish-swish of a chopper and sure enough it slowed down and hovered above the tree. Then there were some very tense moments because there was a strong crosswind that made it hard for the pilot to hold the aircraft in position for the rescue. Finally the winds let up enough so that the chopper could maneuver the basket in place. Woofer heard the funny whirring noise of an electric winch and looked up in time to see a basket being lowered to his spot in the tree. He was afraid to let go of his limb to get in the basket.

Woofer had no idea of what that silly looking tin bird would do to him if it got close enough. They hoisted the basket back up, then lowered it back down with a soldier inside to lift him in. By that time there were droves of people watching the excitement and Woofer gritted his teeth and held his breath while the chopper did it's worst. The family parents were in the crowd but they didn't realize that

Woofer was the one needing help. As the basket was being raised again the mother saw Woofer and began laughing and crying, like mothers will do. Poor Woofer thought "Man, my goose is cooked for sure this time". In a few moments our hero was safe and sound, and back on solid ground with those who loved him and whom he loved in return. When the rescuer handed Woofer to the family he was so excited he wet on the man's shoes.

Trapped in a Tunnel

One day the kids took Woofer along on an adventure viewing the site of an old abandoned mining tunnel. The entrance had been boarded up to keep the local kids and animals safe from harm if they tried to go inside. Over the years the boards had decayed so that they didn't provide enough protection and Woofer managed to squeeze past the barricade and go in anyhow. In the process a rockslide came down, blocking access or escape by covering the entrance to the tunnel, with Woofer trapped inside. Woofer could hear the kids yelling at him from outside and he was casually wondering how in the devil he was going to get out of this fine pickle. He figured he should try to get the kids to think about getting their father to help with his rescue. The kids suddenly thought to call their dad at work for help in saving their beloved mutt. After they described the situation their father brought a back-hoe out from work and in almost no time he had the opening cleared.

As soon as Woofer could claw his way out of the tunnel he high-tailed it for the backhoe and gave the kid's father his most urgent plea for a ride. The father let Woofer ride with him on the machine while he filled the tunnel up with several loads of rock to prevent future danger to others. The father was the pride of the community for his good deeds, including making the old mine safe. Woofer nearly wore his tongue out licking everyone's faces to show his gratitude for being rescued again. Woofer thought, "I'm the only dog in the world with such a terrific family and I thank my lucky stars that they are always on my side". That evening the entire family played Frisbee until it was too dark to see where the thing had gone. Woofer thought "The good old days are right now".

Chased by a Bear

This time Woofer and the kids were playing around near the local dump. They weren't prohibited from going there but they had been cautioned about the dangers of being hurt by items left laying around, as well as by the bears that often went there to scavenge for food. The kids were having a great time pawing through the nameless treasures to be found in the dump but they hadn't thought to wonder about Woofer's whereabouts and they should have realized that things were much too quiet. Woofer watched the kids for awhile until he figured they would be OK if he disappeared to look around. He thought, "Those kids are too busy trying to get themselves in trouble to even think about good old Woofer."

He was curious about some strange noises he heard just above the dump. It sounded like there was something crashing through the brush and it sounded like something awfully big. He climbed upon an old pine stump for a better look, then suddenly he slipped and fell off of the stump with a loud crash. Just then he saw two heads come up out of the bushes. WOW! They were bears! Woofer would have been history except that the bears had a hard time getting out of the brush to chase him.

Meanwhile the kids were playing with some old pots and pans they had found, when there was a sudden loud commotion and Woofer began howling for dear life and running toward them. He was being chased by a bear that looked about twenty feet tall. The bear was gaining two steps to their one and the kids began banging the utensils together as loudly as they could, in the hopes of frightening the beast. It worked, the bear couldn't stand the noise so he turned tail and ran. He was worried about why the other bear had not been in on the chase. Woofer snuggled up tightly at the kids' feet where he felt sure that the bears couldn't get close enough to cause him any harm. The kids were scared out of their wits and Woofer was terrified just to think of what could have happened. The three of them headed for home and the love of the rest of the family. At least he didn't have to lick so many faces that time. Woofer thought he sure was lucky to have so many wonderful people in his life. He thought, "Those darn giants could have had me for hamburger, and then maybe they would have eaten the kids!"

Caught in Two Hunters' Crossfire

Woofer's people lived out in the country where there were miles of beautiful forested areas that the family loved to spend a lot of their free time in just enjoying nature. It was always the highlight of Woofer's times when he was included in the chance to enjoy nature in its finest hour. Much to their dismay someone in the area had been poaching deer in the woods near where Woofer had been trapped in the tree and the police had been trying for months to catch the lawbreakers. The poachers' vehicle tracks were quite familiar to the lawmen and on this occasion they knew their quarry were nearby so they set up a stakeout where they expected the vandals to poach more game.

In the meantime Woofer and the kids were in the blackberry patch hunting berries when all of a sudden they heard loud gunfire and bullets were coming at them from two directions!. Woofer tried his best to get the kids to get down out of sight before they got shot but they didn't even seem to notice. They yelled at the top of their lungs for someone to stop shooting, then the poachers stopped firing. The poachers yelled for the kids to "Get the heck out of there!" During the commotion the police worked their way up behind the poachers and yelled "Drop your weapons and lay flat on the ground!" The kids were too terrified to talk and Woofer didn't even bark, but they were all O.K.

The police took the outlaws into custody without difficulty, along with two freshly killed deer and video film of the violators' actions for evidence so they had a good day. Woofer was beside himself with joy as soon as he was sure the kids were unharmed. Woofer and the kids had a good day. That left the poachers, they had a bad day for a great many days. They were the guests of the local jail for a few months and Woofer had the chance for many great rounds of Frisbee with the family he loved so dearly. He thought, "I should be about due for a break from everything going wrong for a while."

Woofer Fell into a Cistern

The family depended on a well for their household water supply most of the year, however sometimes during droughts the well ran dry and they had a cistern for a backup source for the purpose. When Woofer learned about the cistern and the emergency water supply he thought "This is the dandiest idea I've ever seen. Even if they run clear out of water they still have plenty". The cistern was located under an outbuilding and was used to collect runoff rainwater for use when needed. Water was supplied from the cistern to the house by an electric motor driven pump, but water for livestock was dipped through a trapdoor in the floor with a bucket.

It was one of the times when the well was dry and water was being obtained from the cistern. The kids had watered the animals but they had forgot to close the trapdoor. The family parents happened to be in town on an errand so the kids were less vigilant than usual about their chores. Sure enough, somehow Woofer had managed to fall into the cistern. He started to howl like bloody murder, like the time when he was trapped in the tree and yelped until the kids came to his aid. Woofer was thinking, "This is just my darned rotten luck! It would serve me right if they didn't manage to get my worthless hide out of this scrape."

Again Woofer was thinking how awful it would be if all of the other dogs in the country learned about his stupid predicament. As it turned out, things came pretty close to working out just that way. The kids lacked two or three feet of reaching him, so they tried to rescue him with a rope. They couldn't tie the rope to him or lasso him, but finally they thought of their father's fish net on a hoop and a long pole that he used to land large fish, on lucky days. On the very first try the net went over Woofer's head and down over his body. They lifted him out as easy as pie, then closed the trapdoor and *locked* it. Woofer showed his appreciation by shaking water all over them. About then the parents came back to the ranch, just in time to be greeted by a soaking wet dog. The kids were spared the experience of being punished because things had worked out so well but Woofer thought "I was really scared for them this time. If something had happened to me their misery would have been my fault".

Woofer Broke Through the Ice

Sometimes in the winter it was cold enough for the river to freeze over so thick that people could walk or skate on it. When bodies of water are frozen over, there are often soft spots in the ice caused by warmer areas in the water. The soft spots are a great danger to people and animals because they usually can't be seen. On this occasion the weather was starting to get warmer and the ice was nearly ready to thaw. The kids had been cautioned to stay away from the ice. No one had told Woofer. It was like Murphy's Law, if there's any way possible for something to happen, sooner or later it is bound to happen. Yep, good old Woofer crossed the river, almost.

One of the neighbors heard his pitiful whining and called the family, then headed for the scene. They tried a rope but that idea was no more successful there than it had been at the cistern. A long ladder was just the trick, except that it sank through the soft ice. Just then the father drove right up to the river bank, jumped out and left the pickup running. He jumped in the river with all of his clothes on and easily broke the ice all of the way to the dog. He swam back to the bank with one hand while holding Woofer with the other hand. Woofer and the father were half drowned and half frozen but that was all in the day's work for each of them. The father hugged Woofer longer and harder than anyone else and the dog put his cold, wet head in a nice warm, dry lap for the ride home in his pickup. The father was the pride of the county and was worshiped by the family which included Woofer.

Woofer Gets Snake Bitten

Usually Woofer was very obedient and easy to train except for his fondness for playing with snakes. He didn't seem to care if they were large, small or butt ugly; he liked snakes. Each family member had tried to dissuade him from toying with them, to no avail. He would grab a snake by any part of its body and toss it up in the air, or pull it like a kid's toy wagon by the tail. If no one interfered he would continue this grisly game for hours on end. It seems doubtful that the snake got much enjoyment out of Woofer's pleasure but he didn't seem to be bothered by facts. The father had said that he dreaded the time when Woofer got hold of a rattlesnake.

The dreaded event happened at the family's Fourth of July picnic. After everyone had feasted to their heart's content they played Frisbee for awhile then enjoyed some volleyball and basketball. Then the mother mentioned that she had smuggled in some mincemeat pie, which they all dearly loved. While they were busy with the treats Woofer suddenly began his most dreadful howl, which made the hair stand out on the back of people's necks like cactus thorns. He ran to the group with a snake hanging from his leg. The father quickly killed the snake and rushed Woofer to the vet's home. He dreaded the thought that the vet might be gone for the holiday but he thanked God when he found the man at home. The vet treated the dog and kept him at his home for a few days to be sure he was fully recovered. Woofer was quite sick for a couple of days but then he was nearly recovered and was licking faces again as if nothing had happened. The vet brought Woofer home but flatly refused to accept pay for the dog's treatment and board. He said the dog's company was all of the payment he had any need for. At that point the mother refused to tolerate such behavior and forced him to eat a slice of her famous apple pie. The man was also rewarded by the chance for a few games of Frisbee with his new hero.

Buried in a Snow Bank

After the spring thaw the river was free of ice and the grass was starting to come up and add a bright, cheerful green cast to the area. Mother nature had a surprise message for everyone in that part of the country. Winter wasn't over yet. They had a freak snowstorm that dumped over two feet of snow on the ground. Woofer loved to play in the nice fresh snow so he was up and about early the next morning. It was a beautiful day, the sun was shining brightly and the birds were singing. Then as luck would have it, Murphy's Law struck again. Woofer found a way to burrow in the snow until he couldn't move any farther and nearly suffocated before he was missed. He really was scared that time. He thought "Please don't let me die like this! I want to help the family raise their kids and teach them what they should and shouldn't do with their lives."

The kids saw his tracks in the back yard as they were leaving for school and they noticed that the tracks went about halfway to the gate and stopped! They knew that wasn't right so they got a snow scoop and dug their way along where he had burrowed until they came to the back end of a nearly done-for dog. The kids said, "Please dear Lord, let our dearest Woofer be O.K." Again, Woofer was spared simply because it wasn't his time to go, and because of the family's love and devotion. By the time they got Woofer thawed out and breathing normally again the kids were hours late for school but they had no trouble getting their mother to write an excuse. Later the teacher had no qualms about accepting the excuse because that dog had befriended her time and again. Woofer even let the kids toss his Frisbee a few times to show how pleased he was with their efforts.

Lightning Struck the Doghouse

Woofer usually slept on one of his throw rugs on the front porch but occasionally he slept in his doghouse in the back yard. He could be anywhere outdoors and if there was thunder and lightning he would get scared and run for the doghouse. In the late summer when it was hot and humid he often found a need to scamper for his haven from nature's fury. This time it was getting dark and ominous early in the afternoon and soon there was terrible thunder and lightening. Suddenly Woofer's doghouse shook like it was hit by a train and Woofer smelled smoke! He ran for the house at full speed, howling for dear life. He was shaking so violently that it was a miracle that he didn't faint on the spot. The kids heard him and were running to his rescue when they smelled smoke. The doghouse was actually on fire and the lightning had burned a large crease across the roof and down the side of Woofer's home. The kids put the fire out with the garden hose and calmed Woofer down by petting him and throwing his Frisbee a few times. Woofer's eternal smile regained full brilliance and they were all a happy family again.

WOOFER HELPS OTHERS

After giving the reader a picture of a family pet that is always in trouble and seemingly never provides any service to other beings, it seems fitting to mention that Woofer never was a "user." In fact the following episodes clearly show that his pendulum swings both ways.

Woofer Runs For Someone Else's Dear Life

Once Woofer was sleeping on the front porch and didn't hear the kids leave for the river. It was a very warm day and beautiful outdoors so they had decided to go swimming. They knew the dog was sleeping and figured he would be O.K. where he was. They were taking turns diving off of the river bank until one of them dived into a water-soaked log under the water. The other kid got scared when the first one didn't come back up. On the second rescue dive he found the injured swimmer and towed him to the surface. The kids had been taught CPR in school but this time it simply didn't work. Meanwhile Woofer suddenly awoke and realized that something was terribly wrong. He quickly found their trail and followed them to the river. As he approached them the kid who was O.K. yelled **"Get our dad!"** Woofer ran the four miles to the father's work, then yelped and pulled at the man's pants leg until he got him to come to the rescue. The man grabbed a two-way radio and madly drove to the house with Woofer, then followed the dog to the river. He called the Fire Department with panic in his voice and assisted with the CPR effort.

After what must have seemed like years the rescue team arrived and immediately took the child to the hospital. In the Emergency Room they managed to revive the youngster but they said it was up in the air whether he would survive. The doctor said they got enough water out of the kid's lungs to "Sink a Battleship". The next morning to their surprise the child woke up and asked for Woofer. Before long all was well and the doctor said they could all go home and free up a hospital bed. When they got home Woofer ran to the back yard and ran for his Frisbee, which the others took turns throwing. By then even the mother was getting quite well experienced with the Frisbee. All was well except that Woofer looked like six miles of bad fence.

The Barn is on Fire!

One afternoon after the father returned from work he remarked to the mother that things seemed too peaceful around the place. He said he always felt uneasy in that situation because it was seldom long before the next calamity. His fears were soon justified. After supper they played Frisbee with Woofer for a couple of hours before going to bed. Sometime in the middle of the night the father thought that he heard the horses whinnying in the barn but he guessed it was his imagination so he went back to sleep. Shortly afterward Woofer started barking his loudest and most unnerving bark. Upstairs one of the kids yelled, "The barn is on fire! It looks like the whole thing is a goner!" The whole house was instantly in a state of total disruption. With about three words from the father, calm and order were restored. Everyone remembered what they had been taught in case of emergencies. Each person had been assigned chores and had been trained in doing their job. Within about two minutes everyone was fighting fire and saving animals in their pajamas and slippers. Even Woofer was on hand to herd animals to their corner of the field and hold them there as soon as they were out of their buildings. Woofer worked like magic, not even a chicken escaped his eye or his control. No creature was any the worse for wear than some coughing or wheezing. By morning all of the livestock were fully recovered. The barn roof needed total replacement and the back wall had some scorched boards but there were no other ill affects. Woofer quickly reversed a terrible catastrophe by awakening the group and contributed greatly to the well being of the animals while the people were fighting fire and getting animals out of the buildings. Woofer was lavishly rewarded by a whole evening of Frisbee chasing. He thought "It can't get much better than this!"

A FEW CLOSING REMARKS

People should always be kind to their pets. Someone once said "Anyone who don't spoil their dog ain't worth killin'!" Animals who know they are really loved are loving, loyal and protective of their loved ones. This is believed to apply to all kinds of animals, not just dogs. One might not relish the thought of being affectionate to a rat or an opossum but they all seem to crave love and affection. It is well established that dogs, cats and horses love petting and attention from their human friends. Also many people get great pleasure from making their pets happy. Do yourself a favor, get a pet and do your best to make it's life wonderful. The person who said persons who don't spoil their pets, "aint worth killin'," also said calling dogs man's best friend is, "the understatement of a lifetime."

ABOUT THE AUTHOR

Perry Charles Dodge was born on June 23rd, 1931 at Prairie City, Oregon. He grew up at his grand parents' gold mines in eastern Oregon.

He worked on cattle ranches, logged, mined and worked as a carpenter's helper, then helped build and test race cars, and serviced crop-dusting aircraft. He served twenty-two years in the Air Force as an aircraft electrician.

After the service he worked for fifteen years for the Federal Reserve Bank in Portland, Oregon. He operated a handyman service and a dog kennel. At age 63 he retired to write short stories and his autobiography.

Printed in the United States
1033400004B/304-306